THE SOUL FELT ITS WORTH

A 25-DAY DEVOTIONAL JOURNEY THROUGH THE MUSIC OF CHRISTMAS

CAMERON FRANK

PRESTON NORMAN

Foreword by

NATHAN DRAKE

Published by Cameron Frank in the United States of America.

Published with A Frank Voice

www.afrankvoice.com

Cover Design: Cameron Frank

ISBN:

Paperback: 9798766435655

Claim Your Free Devotional Gift

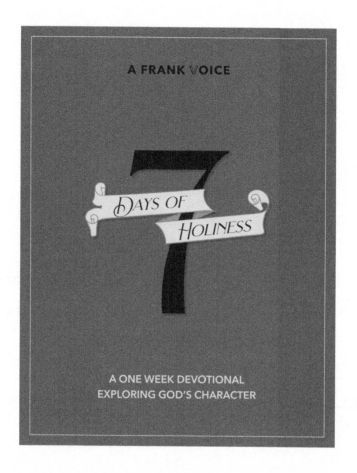

Transform the Way You See Holiness

Claim your **free** *7 Days of Holiness* devotional
from A Frank Voice at
www.7daysofholiness.com

Why stop at reading the lyrics?

Listen to the music of *The Soul Felt Its Worth*, arranged and performed by Nathan Drake of Reawaken Hymns.

Find the album wherever you listen to music.

For a truly unique and powerful experience, find the audiobook at your favorite audiobook retailer and enjoy the music and narration of this devotional in one incredible package.

Visit **www.thesoulfeltitsworth.com** for more.

Publisher's note: there may be differences between the printed lyrics of the hymns in this devotional and the recorded music for the audiobook and album.

FOREWORD

NATHAN DRAKE

It happens at least once a month. I will be minding my own business, thinking not about pine trees or mangers or whatever a sugarplum actually is, and then it happens. Something small—a smell, a feeling, a melody, a large man in a red shirt—will bring about a sudden onrush of joy as Christmas hijacks my every sense, followed almost immediately by an equally sudden, though entirely predictable disappointment that it is not, in fact, Christmas.

It happened again when I picked up this book. Although the reason here is no mystery. More than candles, pine trees, presents, or sugarplums (still no idea), it's the music that connects christmas to the soul.

As I write this, it is the middle of August in St. Louis. The high today is 95 and the humidity could kill a small hippopotamus. But as I sit in my basement, Christmas lights haphazardly strung around my recording studio, It might as well be snowing outside.

I've been in the studio everyday recording all 25 Christmas carols for "The Soul Felt Its Worth" audiobook. Cameron and Preston contacted me a few months prior with the idea for a musical audiobook version of the devotional you are holding right now. They may have asked me because I've spent the last 5 years creating simple, modern versions of hymns through the worship resource I created, "Reawaken Hymns". Though the more likely reason is that no one else in the continental United States was unwell enough to try to record 25 christmas carols in a month.

At this point I've "listened" to the songs hundreds of times. I've said the words "peace" and "goodwill" more than "hello" or "yes, I know it's only August". Yet, everytime I hit the play button on one of these carols, that feeling is still there. You know the one. That strange mix of nostalgia, warmth, joy, and mild panic.

That's what Christmas music does. It connects us to the story, the emotions, the truths. And it does so in a way that only music can. Bringing the intangible to life through music. And it does something else amazing, too. It leaves the church.

For an entire month, the secular and Christian worlds join together to set their minds on whatever is true, whatever is honorable, whatever is just, whatever is pure, whatever is lovely, whatever is commendable.

And that's what this book is about.

The classic Christmas carols aren't just the nativity set to music, they are a means to dwell on all things good in our world.

Peace on earth.
    Goodwill to men.
    The wrong shall fail.
    The right prevail

Joy to the world.

Right now you are holding a means to dwell on all things good. The reason we celebrate the arrival of our Christ in a manger is because that arrival ushered in the beginning of the Kingdom of all things good.

In this book, Cameron and Preston have given you 25 days of what is true, what is honorable, what is just, what is pure, what is lovely, what is commendable, what is Christmas. All you have to do is dwell.

Nathan Drake
    Reawaken Hymns

INTRODUCTION

I love Christmas. My closest friends and family know that I start listening to Christmas music well before the weather changes. There is such a joy and jubilee in Christmas music. I admit that there's also a healthy dose of nostalgia that lends to my love of the season and the whole atmosphere of the holiday.

It's the entire experience: Christmas movies, music, decorations, the chill in the air, the memories, wrapping paper—it's hard to isolate just one part of the season that really makes it. But one of the most important aspects of

Christmas to me is that we celebrate one of the two most pivotal events in human history.

The second event is Easter, where we celebrate and rejoice at the resurrection of Jesus, when He conquered sin and death once and for all. But for Jesus to live a perfect life and die on the cross for us and be resurrected in victory, He first must have been born. To quote Linus Van Pelt, "That's what Christmas is all about, Charlie Brown."

We'll look at Christmas carols that instantly take us back to our childhood. They have a special way of drawing on nostalgia and filling us with the childhood joy of Christmas. Sometimes we'll be transported back to children's choirs, dressing in a bedsheet to play a shepherd with the cartoon camels.

We'll look at some more obscure selections that are no less powerful—no less impactful and theologically rich. We'll dive into verses that have since faded from popular usage, but paint incredible pictures of the human condition and Christ's redeeming love for us.

It can be easy to forget why we celebrate,

why we rejoice, and what the season is really all about in the midst of festivities, traditions, shopping, parties, family, and everything else that goes on during this time of year. Sure, we all *know* that Christmas is about Jesus. It's right there in the name, after all. But do we really *feel* it? In the busyness of the season, do we take the time to truly soak in the powerful truth of how God stepped into the world to save us from sin and death?

Our prayer for this book is that it will help you do just that—take time to soak in that truth.

Over the next 25 days, we'll look at prayers of longing, hymns of remembrance, and songs of hope. We'll dive into the Scriptures and study what the coming of the Christ means for us each and every day, not only for the Christmas season.

If you're going through this with your family or a small group, we encourage you to discuss the questions and use them as an opportunity for reflection and vulnerability. This can be a time to share, embrace, and encourage one another. We've included plenty of blank space so that you can write in answers to the questions if you choose.

Our hope for this devotional is for it to be a cry of joyful expectation and a rejoicing of God's people at His faithfulness and provision. We want this time to be a break from the busyness of the Christmas season and a time to reflect on the promises and provision of God.

When the Creator stepped down into creation in the ultimate act of sacrificial love, the Holy became the meek and the soul felt its worth.

DECEMBER 1ST

COME THOU FOUNT OF EVERY BLESSING

Come, Thou Fount of every blessing
Tune my heart to sing Thy grace
Streams of mercy, never ceasing
Call for songs of loudest praise
Teach me some melodious sonnet
Sung by flaming tongues above
Praise the mount, I'm fixed upon it
Mount of Thy redeeming love

Here I raise my Ebenezer
Here there by Thy great help I've come
And I hope, by Thy good pleasure
Safely to arrive at home

Jesus sought me when a stranger
Wandering from the fold of God
He, to rescue me from danger
Interposed His precious blood

Oh, that day when freed from sinning
I shall see Thy lovely face
Clothed then in the blood washed linen
How I'll sing Thy wondrous grace
Come, my Lord, no longer tarry
Take my ransomed soul away
Send Thine angels now to carry
Me to realms of endless day

Oh, to grace how great a debtor
Daily I'm constrained to be
Let that goodness like a fetter
Bind my wandering heart to Thee
Prone to wander, Lord, I feel it
Prone to leave the God I love
Here's my heart, oh, take and seal it
Seal it for Thy courts above

HISTORY

This is one of my favorite hymns. I've never really considered it a Christmas song, but in preparing for this devotional and browsing lists of Christmas hymns, this gem popped up more than once. That was all the permission I needed to include this favorite hymn of mine.

It's not as if it doesn't fit, however. The themes of Christ's arrival and purpose of redemption are so present in the words, it's no wonder it is often included in Christmas collections. It makes a great prayer for us as we enter this Christmas season.

In 1758, a recently converted believer and soon-to-be Baptist preacher named Robert Robinson wrote the words to this beloved hymn. Around 15 years prior, his mother sent him to be an apprentice after his father had died. Without any real guidance or parentage, he quickly fell into a worldly lifestyle, finding himself involved with notorious street gangs and all manner of depravity.

When he was 20 years old, Robert heard George Whitefield's preaching and the Lord brought him back into the fold. The rawness and reality of his prodigal history is palpable in lines like, "Jesus sought me when a stranger, wandering from the fold of God," and "Prone to wander, Lord, I feel it, prone to leave the God I love."

Robert would go on to pastor a Baptist church for almost three decades. For nearly 300 years, this hymn has been treasured in churches around the world as a bold proclamation of Christ's pursuit of us. This is a powerful truth we can soak in not only during the Christmas season, but it's applicable every day.

DEVOTION

From creation to God's providence in the wilderness—manna and water for the wandering nation of Israel—to His faithfulness in the exile, His continually poured out blessing was all leading toward this moment: the coming of the King.

The "Ebenezer" that Robinson references in the second verse refers to 1 Samuel 7:12 and the stone of remembrance that Samuel erected as a testament to God's deliverance. A great place to start this Christmas season is to remember that it's all about Jesus coming in meek power to rescue us and deliver us from our sin.

It's about deliverance—everything in all of creation leads us to the coming of our Savior. Ephesians 1:7-10 says, "In him we have redemption through his blood, the forgiveness of our trespasses, according to the riches of his grace, which he lavished upon us, in all wisdom and insight making known to us the mystery of his will, according to his purpose, which he set forth in Christ as a plan for the fullness of time, to unite all things in him, things in heaven and things on earth."

What is the plan? To bring us all back to Him. Even when we don't deserve it. Robert Robinson wrote, "Jesus sought me when a stranger, wandering from the fold of God," which is a powerful reminder of how good our God is. Romans 5:8 reminds us that, "while we were still sinners, Christ died for us."

From the very first sin, the plan was always to reconcile us back to Him. 2000 years ago, when Jesus came, that plan was born to a virgin in a manger, and it's that plan we celebrate.

APPLICATION

This time of year, it's all about the hustle and bustle. There's shopping, decorating, Christmas parties, family, and all the things we love about this season. All of these can be great things, but we must not forget why we celebrate. Take a moment today and pray for a dose of supernatural remembrance.

We see a powerful truth reflected in this hymn: we ought to pray with a boldness born of remembrance. We should pray with the bold expectation that God will move. Let us not forget that even as we pray for blessing, we remember just how much He *has* blessed us. That ought to change the way you pray.

God has provided a path to salvation

through the blood of His Son! Do you know that He saved *you?* Yes, you! The power of the Gospel is that Christ died for us, and that "whoever believes in him might not perish, but have eternal life." (John 3:16) God has brought new life to dead vessels, and it all starts here. It starts with belief and remembering that the fount of every blessing has indeed come.

So here's your homework: build a stone of remembrance. You don't have to literally build a monument (though I'm not one to discourage you) but set something in place to help you remember God's blessing—and let that breed boldness in you. Thank God for His awesome purpose and plan. Thank Him for sending His Son and ask Him to help you focus on what Christmas is all about.

SCRIPTURE READING

James 1:16-18; 22-25, Romans 5, Ephesians 1:3-10

QUESTIONS

1. Reflect on how God has blessed you in the most powerful way; what is your salvation testimony?
2. Why do you think we're so prone to wander?
3. How will you set a "stone of remembrance" that will help you better remember God's deliverance?

DECEMBER 2ND

O COME O COME EMMANUEL

O come, O come, Emmanuel,
And ransom captive Israel,
That mourns in lonely exile here,
Until the Son of God appear.
Rejoice! Rejoice! Emmanuel
Shall come to thee, O Israel.

O come, Thou Rod of Jesse, free
Thine own from Satan's tyranny;
From depths of hell Thy people save,
And give them victory o'er the grave.
Rejoice! Rejoice! Emmanuel
Shall come to thee, O Israel.

O come, Thou Dayspring, from on high,
And cheer us by Thy drawing nigh;
Disperse the gloomy clouds of night,
And death's dark shadows put to flight.
Rejoice! Rejoice! Emmanuel
Shall come to thee, O Israel.

O come, Thou Key of David, come
And open wide our heav'nly home;
Make safe the way that leads on high,
And close the path to misery.
Rejoice! Rejoice! Emmanuel
Shall come to thee, O Israel.

O come, Adonai, Lord of might,
Who to Thy tribes, on Sinai's height,
In ancient times didst give the law
In cloud and majesty and awe.
Rejoice! Rejoice! Emmanuel
Shall come to thee, O Israel.

HISTORY

There are many claims that the words to this hymn were penned as early as the 12th century, but the oldest surviving original Latin form dates back to 1710. It is based on the O Antiphons, which were common chants from early Christians that denoted Christ's names (and His corresponding attributes). As such, this hymn is Biblically rich and resonates echoes of liturgy from our spiritual ancestors.

Each line of the O Antiphons refers back to a prophecy from Isaiah which describes an attribute of Jesus with a name. The rich history of the O Antiphons dates all the way back at least to the late fifth or early sixth centuries, and possibly earlier. For over 1,500 years in some way or other, reciting the names of Jesus has been a significant part of Christian liturgy. We get to share a powerful legacy with our brothers and sisters in Christ from centuries past through hymns like this.

Our modern versions of the song typically include anywhere from three to six verses, with names including: Emmanuel, Adonai (Lord of might), Rod of Jesse, Dayspring, Desire of nations, Key of David, and Wisdom.

DEVOTION

"Our help is in the name of the LORD, who made heaven and earth." (Psalm 124:8)

The names of Jesus juxtaposed with the somber tones of longing serve as a powerful reminder: though our circumstances change and trials and tribulations arise, God never changes and His faithfulness is constant. Why are names important? Names reflect identity. The names of God describe the attributes of God, and just as His names don't change, His attributes don't change.

For you, this season may be a time marked more by sorrow than joyful expectation. This could be your first Christmas without your mom. This could be another year without a child. Maybe as your children wonder about gifts, it's another reminder that you haven't been able to find a job.

Though the world around you may seem to be in flux, the one thing that never changes is who God is. Whatever the cause for sorrow, know this: in Jesus there is hope. His name hasn't changed and He never changes. His love is constant and His blessings flow without ceasing. That is where our hope comes from this Christmas season.

APPLICATION

It's okay to mourn. It's okay to struggle. In your longing, turn to the God who is with us. When the birth of Jesus was foretold in Isaiah 7:14, the prophet says the name of Jesus will be Immanuel, which means God with us. Him being with us is a part of His unchanging nature. In His name, there is deliverance, peace, rescue, might, and wisdom. Maybe this holiday season, you simply need to lean on those truths.

In Yellowstone National Park there is a famous geyser named "Old Faithful." It was named that way in 1870 when explorers noted the regularity of the geyser. It earned its name by a pattern of consistent behavior that proved its character. Jesus is named "God with us" and we can trust in that name because it is born of a pattern of faithfulness.

In sorrow, in doubt, in turmoil, and in joy, God is with us. How life-giving is that? Trust in that name. The faithfulness of God's presence in our lives has been proven time and time again. He is with us through difficulty and with us through joy. What hope we have! Through it all, in the name of Jesus, don't forget to rejoice! Because God has come to us. That is where our hope comes from.

SCRIPTURE READING

Psalm 136, Matthew 1:18-23, Isaiah 7:14

QUESTIONS

1. How does reflecting on the names of Jesus give you hope?
2. Where does your hope come from?
3. This song compels us to rejoice because Immanuel has come. Describe a few reasons you can rejoice today.

DECEMBER 3RD

COME THOU LONG EXPECTED JESUS

Come, thou long expected Jesus,
born to set thy people free;
from our fears and sins release us,
let us find our rest in thee.
Israel's strength and consolation,
hope of all the earth thou art;
dear desire of every nation,
joy of every longing heart.

Born thy people to deliver,
born a child and yet a King,
born to reign in us forever,
now thy gracious kingdom bring.

By thine own eternal spirit
rule in all our hearts alone;
by thine all sufficient merit,
raise us to thy glorious throne.

HISTORY

This hymn was written in 1744 by the great hymnist, Charles Wesley. As he meditated on Haggai 2:7, he noted the tragic orphan situation in Great Britain, as well as the great class divide of the time. In 18th century England, orphaned children were taken advantage of in terrible ways. Not only was there an epidemic of homeless children, but the so-called orphanages that housed the children were orphanages in name only. More accurately, they were "workhouses."

Children were forced into doing the kinds of manual labor no one else wanted to do. They were often beaten, starved, and otherwise mistreated in unimaginable ways. It was this heartbreaking world that Wesley saw around him.

Everywhere he looked, it seemed, there was injustice.

He penned this hymn as a hymn of hope and expectation—the groanings of humanity have for so long expected our Savior to return and set all things right. This is a hymn of remembrance for us *and* an anthem of eager anticipation. We remember that Jesus came in the humblest form, yet full of glory, and we eagerly long for His final return.

DEVOTION

Psalm 34 is a great anthem for God's people as we long for deliverance from the injustices of the world. Verse 18 promises that "The LORD is near to the brokenhearted and saves the crushed in spirit."

Many of the same injustices that plagued those in Charles Wesley's day still afflict those around the modern world. We are still longing for the final return of Christ, but as David boldly declares in Psalm 34:1, "I will bless the

LORD at all times; his praise shall continually be in my mouth."

Regardless of our circumstance, we know that the Lord is good. He is our deliverer. He is the defender of the brokenhearted and Savior of the crushed in spirit. It's easy to look around at the terrors that sin throws at our world every single day—five minutes watching the news is more than enough to see how much creation groans for redemption. The more we see, the easier it is to wonder where God is and when He will bring a final end to the trouble.

But we know His promises are true and faithful. How do we know? He promised to send a Savior to redeem people to Him, and 2,000 years ago He did exactly that. The long-expected Jesus came as a humble child, but saved the nations. That same Savior promised that He would return.

APPLICATION

God is a keeper of promises. He has shown His faithfulness time and time again. As the little orphan Annie might say, you can bet your bottom dollar on that.

So as we look around at the injustice of the world, what do we do? We exalt the Lord, even though it may be hard to see His plan. We bless Him every day. We call out to Him and trust that He is near to the brokenhearted.

We long for the return of Jesus, but in the meantime, we have a job to do. He has left us here to do His work. Micah 6:8 illustrates this command for us in unambiguous terms: "He has told you, O man, what is good; and what does the LORD require of you but to do justice, and to love kindness, and to walk humbly with your God?"

This Christmas season, look for ways to bless the Lord by blessing people. We're put here to put others first, and there's no greater time to do that than this time of year.

SCRIPTURE READING

Psalm 34, Psalm 126

QUESTIONS

1. What are some injustices you see every day?
2. What are some ways other people have blessed you in times of need or hardship?
3. What can you do to help defend the brokenhearted and crushed in spirit?

DECEMBER 4TH

IT CAME UPON THE MIDNIGHT CLEAR

It came upon the midnight clear,
That glorious song of old,
From angels bending near the earth,
To touch their harps of gold:
"Peace on the earth, goodwill to men,
From heaven's all-gracious King."
The world in solemn stillness lay,
To hear the angels sing.

Yet with the woes of sin and strife
The world has suffered long;
Beneath the angel-strain have rolled
Two thousand years of wrong;

And man, at war with man, hears not
The love-song which they bring;
O hush the noise, ye men of strife,
And hear the angels sing.

And ye, beneath life's crushing load,
Whose forms are bending low,
Who toil along the climbing way
With painful steps and slow,
Look now! for glad and golden hours
come swiftly on the wing.
O rest beside the weary road,
And hear the angels sing!

For lo!, the days are hastening on,
By prophet bards foretold,
When with the ever-circling years
Comes round the age of gold
When peace shall over all the earth
Its ancient splendors fling,
And the whole world give back the song
Which now the angels sing.

When Edmund Sears penned these somber words in 1849, it seemed that so much of his nation was wrapped up in turmoil. Fresh from the wounds of the brutal Mexican-American war, with the whispers of civil war looming on the horizon, the writer wonders where this peace that was promised is. As he laments how much we've missed the point, you can almost hear him crying, "Jesus our Savior has come, but we're warring over something as petty and worldly as land?"

The song itself is based on the depiction of the angels singing "Peace on earth," from Luke 2:14. Most telling of Sears' intent is the third stanza which is missing from many modern hymnals. It is equal parts heartbreaking and conflict-condemning:

> *Yet with the woes of sin and strife*
> *The world has suffered long;*
> *Beneath the angel-strain have rolled*
> *Two thousand years of wrong;*

And man, at war with man, hears not
The love-song which they bring;
hush the noise, ye men of strife,
And hear the angels sing.

DEVOTION

There are a few phrases that innately sound Christmas-y. "Peace on earth, goodwill to men," is one of them, largely due to the popularity of this song. It's a delightful sentiment, though perhaps misguided in the object of its promise.

If you've kept up with current events for more than five minutes recently, "peace" certainly isn't a word that can be used to describe our current state. Far from it. Much like in Sears' time, our world is being ripped apart by strife and petty battles in new and creative ways every day. Where can we find encouragement in this? The answer is in His Word, where Jesus told us it would be like this.

In John 16, Jesus is spending His last precious moments pouring into His disciples and preparing them for His imminent departure.

"Behold, the hour is coming, indeed it has come, when you will be scattered each to his own home, and will leave me alone. Yet I am not alone, for the Father is with me. I have said these things to you, that in me you may have peace. In the world you will have tribulation. But take heart; I have overcome the world."

In Jesus' words, He warns us of despair and tribulation, but He also encourages us: in Him we have peace. We may not have peace from physical trial and tribulation, but we have spiritual peace from the Prince of Peace who died to purchase goodwill for the souls of sinners who believe in Him.

APPLICATION

We sing about peace a lot this time of year, but sometimes that peace is hard to find. From the hustle and bustle of the busy season to the mourning over loss and everything in between, as we sing "peace on the earth," it sometimes feels like more of a hopeful question than a promise.

Remember what happened 2,000 years ago when a Savior was born in a humble manger: a redemptive plan was set in motion that would change the world forever. War and strife and toiling and turmoil would only increase as sin rebelled, but Jesus offers peace in Him.

The angel song in Luke 2 begins with "Glory to God in the highest," and rightly places the emphasis and the heart on the God who provides the final peace. In light of the bigness of God, the small toils of this life only get smaller. This holiday season, set aside time to take Sears' advice: hush the noise and join in the song of peace.

SCRIPTURE READING

John 16:32-33, Isaiah 26:1-12

QUESTIONS

1. What are some "noises" in your life that distract you from the peace God promised?
2. How have you experienced the peace that God's saving grace has brought?
3. What are some steps you can take to promote peace and goodwill in your community of influence?

DECEMBER 5TH

WHILE SHEPHERDS WATCHED
THEIR FLOCKS

While shepherds watched their flocks by
   night,
All seated on the ground,
The angel of the Lord came down,
And glory shone around.

"Fear not!" said he, for mighty dread
Had seized their troubled mind;
"Glad tidings of great joy I bring
To you and all mankind.

"To you, in David's town, this day
Is born of David's line

A Savior, who is Christ the Lord,
And this shall be the sign:

"The heav'nly Babe you there shall find
To human view displayed,
All meanly wrapped in swathing bands,
And in a manger laid."

Thus spake the seraph and forthwith
Appeared a shining throng
Of angels praising God on high,
Who thus addressed their song:

"All glory be to God on high,
And to the Earth be peace;
Good will henceforth from heav'n to men
Begin and never cease!"

HISTORY

The Church of England made this hymn a staple shortly after Nahum Tate wrote it around the year 1700. It's significant for the church because it was the first and only

Christmas carol sanctioned by the church for many years—the Anglicans had only previously sanctioned psalmody.

Psalmody is the practice of singing or chanting the Psalms, with as little alteration to the original text as possible. In the early days of the church, believers would often sing or chant the Psalms as their mode of worship. The early church used no instruments for centuries until after the Protestant Reformation when Lutheran churches in Germany began experimenting with organs and other instruments.

Many of the more conservative Protestant sects held that Psalmody was the only Biblical way to worship. This began to shift in the 1700s as the psalters were updated and new ideas were promoted.

The history for this particular hymn isn't very deep or storied—it is essentially Scripture set to meter. All things considered, it's hard to argue with that.

DEVOTION

Do you ever feel too unusable or unskilled for God to even notice you, much less have a purpose for you? Maybe the circumstances of your life have crippled your self-confidence, or maybe you're just not sure how your talents and abilities can be used to reach the nations for the Gospel.

Can I encourage you with something? God created you for a purpose. He created you with your gifts, talents, and abilities with a purpose and a mission that only *you* can fulfill. Imagine if God was working a puzzle with billions of pieces—He has made each piece unique, and each has a very particular spot in the puzzle that only one piece can fit into. God has made you to fit the exact place He has for you, don't talk yourself out of how important you are.

In Luke 2, God used shepherds to announce the birth of His Son—the most important birth the world has ever seen. Can you imagine? There they were, watching their sheep on the night shift, maybe even trying to help keep each other awake, when all of a sudden the sky rips open and an angel appears before them. Their mission was simple: tell people about it.

Do you remember what happened next? People were amazed at their words. They marveled. They didn't ask what qualifications the shepherds may have had or question them because their skill sets didn't meet expectations.

The power of the Gospel is that it moves people with supernatural grace, and sometimes we get the blessing of being the vessel.

APPLICATION

You are important. You are talented and skilled and we need you in the fight. Yes, you.

God doesn't make useless people. Ephesians 2:10 reminds us that, "We are his workmanship, created in Christ Jesus for good works, which God prepared beforehand, that we should walk in them."

Did you catch that? God has designed all of us to walk in the good works of Christ and has created us to do that in a specific way. It may look different for all of us, but we're set aside for a purpose and to do good works in Jesus' name.

Maybe you're starting to feel the pressures as the end of the year approaches and you didn't finish the goals you planned. Or maybe it's another year gone by and you don't feel like you've made an impact for the Kingdom at all. It's never too late to start. You may not have gotten to every goal you planned, but there's still time to do something that matters. Find what you're good at and what you love to do and do it for the Gospel. Or you can always be like the shepherds and tell people that Jesus has come.

SCRIPTURE READING

Luke 2:8-14, Ephesians 2:8-10; 19-22

QUESTIONS

1. What are some lies the enemy tries to tell you to discourage you about your ability?
2. How can you use your gifts, talents, and abilities to work for the Gospel?

DECEMBER 6TH

O LITTLE TOWN OF BETHLEHEM

O little town of Bethlehem
How still we see thee lie
Above thy deep and dreamless sleep
The silent stars go by
Yet in thy dark streets shineth
The everlasting Light
The hopes and fears of all the years
Are met in thee tonight

For Christ is born of Mary
And gathered all above
While mortals sleep, the angels keep
Their watch of wondering love

O morning stars together
Proclaim the holy birth
And praises sing to God the King
And Peace to men on earth

How silently, how silently
The wondrous gift is given!
So God imparts to human hearts
The blessings of His heaven.
No ear may hear His coming,
But in this world of sin,
Where meek souls will receive him still,
The dear Christ enters in.

O holy Child of Bethlehem
Descend to us, we pray
Cast out our sin and enter in
Be born to us today
We hear the Christmas angels
The great glad tidings tell
O come to us, abide with us
Our Lord Emmanuel

HISTORY

In 1865, on Christmas Eve, a New England pastor named Phillips Brooks made the trek from Jerusalem to Bethlehem on horseback. His entourage passed by the fields from where the shepherds were visited by an angel and through the quiet streets of Bethlehem—then with a population of only 4,000 or so.

Brooks would never be the same. Just a few short years later in the winter of 1868, he wrote a poem with these words, and asked his church's organist to put it to music to be performed with the children's Christmas Sunday school that year. The two men never thought the song would live beyond that Christmas, but over 150 years later, it's still a treasured carol for children and adults alike.

DEVOTION

The town of Bethlehem was small, modest, and unassuming—until it wasn't. In Micah 5, the prophet foretells that Bethlehem, a place "too small to be among the clans of Judah," will deliver unto us a Savior and a Shepherd. Verse 5 of that same chapter delivers a simple hope about the coming Messiah: "And he shall be their peace."

God often uses the smallest vessels for the largest blessings. We can look to Moses, who pleaded with God that he wasn't the right man for the job. Or take Gideon in Judges 7, where God asked Gideon many times to shrink the size of his force before taking on the enemy. It's counter-intuitive, but there is a purpose.

God wants every blessing to point to Him because, after all, all blessings come from Him in the first place. It should come as no surprise that the greatest blessing the world has ever received arrived through humble means, in a humble place, in the form of a humble baby.

That little town of Bethlehem slept on their promise, but God didn't need fanfare. As the carol says, "meek souls will receive Him still," and that's a good reason to rejoice.

APPLICATION

Do you know your purpose? In a broad sense, it is very much the same as anyone else—to preach Christ crucified (1 Corinthians 1:23). How God has created you to fulfill that purpose is something only you can know. Bethlehem had it easy—their fate was foretold about 700 years before it would come to pass.

Whatever the case, never think yourself too small or insignificant to see God's mission fulfilled in you. Don't sleep on the purpose and promise that God has given you.

God delivered a prophecy for Bethlehem 700 years before it would take place, but even then He was working behind the scenes to maneuver the circumstances for His promise to be fulfilled. He does the same thing in each of us. Embrace His promise and His purpose for you today. God never lies and He never leaves a promise hanging.

From the most unassuming place, the Savior of all mankind was born. What can He do in you?

SCRIPTURE READING

Micah 5:1-6, Judges 7:1-9, 1 Corinthians 1:4-9; 26-31

QUESTIONS

1. What is the purpose that all Christians share?
2. How has God uniquely created you to fulfill that purpose in your everyday life?
3. What is a bold step you can take today to trust God's promise in your purpose?

DECEMBER 7TH

ONCE IN ROYAL DAVID'S CITY

Once in royal David's city,
Stood a lowly cattle shed,
Where a mother laid her baby
In a manger for his bed:
Mary was that mother mild,
Jesus Christ her little child.

He came down to earth from heaven
Who is God and Lord of all,
And his shelter was a stable,
And his cradle was a stall;
With the poor and mean and lowly
Lived on earth our Saviour holy.

For he is our childhood's pattern,
Day by day, like us he grew,
He was little, weak and helpless,
Tears and smiles like us he knew:
And he feeleth for our sadness
And he shareth in our gladness.

And our eyes at last shall see him,
Through his own redeeming love,
For that child so dear and gentle
Is our Lord in heaven above;
And he leads his children on
To the place where he is gone.

HISTORY

This is a carol that may be unfamiliar to many of us in America, but is rich with tradition in Great Britain. Originally written as a poem in 1848 by Cecil Frances Alexander, this carol was published in her *Hymns for the Little Children* hymnbook. The intent of the poem and subsequent hymn is to musically teach part of the catechism in a memorable way. Songs and hymns like this were designed to teach the truths of Scripture to children in a way they could commit to memory.

The hymn would later be set to music and 60 years after it was written, it would make the world's stage to launch the Christmas Eve Festival of Nine Lessons and Carols each and every year. Every Christmas Eve since 1919, the Festival of Nine Lessons and Carols has began with this hymn. It is an incredible honor to be selected as the soloist for the first stanza to quite literally sing before the world. Since that very first festival, these words have taught the childhood of Jesus to countless millions and helped to serve as a reminder of Christ's humble beginnings.

The theology is light in much of this carol—and in some places a little loose. Some stanzas have been met with criticism over the years, and though the words to those stanzas make sense in the context of the carol, they still make plenty of assumptions about the childhood of Christ. Even still, it serves as a great way to begin teaching children about Jesus in a way that connects well with them.

DEVOTION

The Bible describes Christ's birth as Jesus having "emptied himself" to be born in the likeness of men. Jesus became as we are: humble and subject to the law. The difference? Jesus was thoroughly untainted by sin, being God in the flesh.

So why would the "light of the world" take the bold step into darkness? The answer is simple, sweet, and life-giving: He loves us.

When Jesus stepped into this world to fulfill the law, it was an unprecedented act of love at odds with logic. Logically, God should have no desire to pour out such a sacrificial love into His rebellious and irreverent people. Love is the only explanation. A deep and meaningful love. A perfect love.

In Galatians 4:4-5, Paul reminds us, "But when the fullness of time had come, God sent forth his Son, born of woman, born under the law, to redeem those who were under the law, so that we might receive adoption as sons."

APPLICATION

So what do we do with this knowledge? How do we respond to this boundless love our Savior has poured out on us by stepping into this world in every kind of humility?

Philippians 2 gives us a little insight: "So at the name of Jesus every knee should bow, in heaven and on earth and under the earth, and every tongue confess that Jesus Christ is Lord, to the glory of God the Father."

Jesus wants us to know Him and trust Him enough to call Him Lord. With such a sacrificial act of love, the trust should come easily. When we trust Him, He transforms us. When we call Him Lord, He leads us and guides us.

Here is the amazing truth: you have been redeemed. Your debt has been purchased by blood. The story of your redemption began with the humble Jesus child and carries on every single day until His return.

SCRIPTURE READING

Philippians 2:4-11, John 1:1-16, Galatians 4:4-7

QUESTIONS

1. What does it mean that Jesus
   humbled Himself?
2. Why is it sometimes hard to trust
   Him, even in light of such sacrificial
   love?
3. What does Jesus' act of sacrificial love
   say about you?

DECEMBER 8TH

LO HOW A ROSE E'ER BLOOMING

Lo, how a Rose e'er blooming
From tender stem hath sprung!
Of Jesse's lineage coming
As men of old have sung.
It came, a flower bright,
Amid the cold of winter
When half-gone was the night.

Isaiah 'twas foretold it,
The Rose I have in mind:
With Mary we behold it,
The virgin mother kind.
To show God's love aright

She bore to men a Savior
When half-gone was the night.

This Flower, whose fragrance tender
With sweetness fills the air,
Dispels with glorious splendor
The darkness everywhere.
True man, yet very God,
From sin and death He saves us
And lightens every load

HISTORY

This is one of the oldest songs in this book. People have been singing this song during the Christmas season for centuries—about four of them, in fact. The earliest example of this hymn in print is two German stanzas from 1599, though some traditions hold that it may date back to Martin Luther's time.

The author's identity, if ever known, has been lost to time. The music for the piece was composed in 1609 and has remained largely unchanged in the centuries since—a fascinating testament to the caliber of the original work.

The lyrics have had many incarnations, all centered around the same themes, but translated through the lenses of Catholicism and Protestantism at different points. Later stanzas have been added as well throughout history. The lyrics included here combine Theodore Baker's translation of the first two verses from 1894 and Harriet Spaeth's translation of a Friedrich Layriz verse from 1844. This is the version you will find in the 2008 Baptist Hymnal.

DEVOTION

This sweet hymn is based on the prophecies of Isaiah referring to the coming of the Christ. It tells of Jesus' lineage through Jesse of Bethlehem and the rose that blossoms in the wilderness. This is symbolic of the drought and withering that sin has brought into the world, both literally in Biblical times, and the metaphorical drought that sin causes in our soul.

Isaiah 33 describes a people crying out to the Lord for rescue from the barrenness of their own disobedience. But in Isaiah 35, we see the promise of God, that "the dry land will be glad; the desert will rejoice and blossom like a wildflower." (CSB)

This flower is a symbol of the coming Christ, a sign of life from death, and a promise of restoration. How beautiful is the first flower of Spring? The first sign of life after a season of death—this paints a beautiful picture of the Gospel. In the wilderness where there is no life, life has been promised.

The redemption and restoration of God's people wasn't something God thought of on the spot with the incarnation of Jesus. The redemptive plan has been in motion since the beginning of time. From the original sin, through the calling of His people and their deliverance in the wilderness, and through the line of David to the blooming of the rose in the wilderness—

Jesus—God's plan has been weaving a path to redemption and bringing life from death.

APPLICATION

Sometimes it's hard to see the plan. It's hard to trust that there is a resolution and light at the end of the tunnel. This world is working against us at every opportunity, and where the world leaves an opening, we have an enemy who strives to accuse us, tempt us, and paralyze us.

But God has a plan. From the dawn of time, He began a good work and began weaving a redemptive narrative to bring a people to Him. His promise to the prophets was fulfilled in the work of Christ, and His promise in the death, burial, and resurrection of Christ is at work each and every day in each of His children.

As the hymn says, "from sin and death he saves us and lightens every load," and what a great encouragement that is! He is our Savior, predicted and foretold. He is our friend and Helper and the promise of Scripture. Don't let the Christmas craziness steal your joy and replace it with stress and worry. We worship a God who has been working an intricate plan with more detail than we can fathom. You are a part of that plan, and He won't let you falter if you call on His name.

SCRIPTURE READING

Isaiah 11:1-11, Isaiah 35, Matthew 11:25-30

QUESTIONS

1. What does the symbolism of life from death in a flower in the wilderness mean to you?
2. How does the prophecy of Jesus provide peace and comfort for us today?
3. What are you holding on to that gets in the way of seeing the purpose and the plan that God has for you?

DECEMBER 9TH

I HEARD THE BELLS ON CHRISTMAS DAY

I heard the bells on Christmas Day
Their old, familiar carols play,
and wild and sweet
The words repeat
Of peace on earth, good-will to men!

And thought how, as the day had come,
The belfries of all Christendom
Had rolled along
The unbroken song
Of peace on earth, good-will to men!

Till ringing, singing on its way,

The world revolved from night to day,
A voice, a chime,
A chant sublime
Of peace on earth, good-will to men!

And in despair I bowed my head;
"There is no peace on earth," I said;
"For hate is strong,
And mocks the song
Of peace on earth, good-will to men!"

Then pealed the bells more loud and deep:
"God is not dead, nor doth He sleep;
The Wrong shall fail,
The Right prevail,
With peace on earth, good-will to men."

HISTORY

Like some other entries in this book, the darker notes of this hymn descend directly from the solemnity born of the American Civil War. Henry Wadsworth Longfellow wrote this poem in the middle of the Civil War on

Christmas Day in 1863. His second wife of 18 years had passed away unexpectedly and his son had gone to fight for the Union army in the war, devastating Longfellow. The poet was an abolitionist, but more than anything wanted peace among the people of his nation.

It would be another ten years before the poem would be set to music by organist John Baptiste Calkin. His tune would become the standard for many years.

More than almost any other Christmas Carol, the words to this poem seem almost at odds with the spirit of Christmas. In fact, even as the poem claims the bells mock the glad tidings, the poem itself seems to make a mockery of the Christmas joy. This comes as no surprise, as Longfellow was writing from a place of unrest.

By the hymn's resolution that those bells don't mock peace, they remind us that "God is not dead," it's almost as if the writer is trying to convince himself of that truth more than anything. Though some artists have tried to add jingle bells and jolly sounds to this somber song, I haven't found that it does the song justice; let the conflict shine and resolution come as "the world revolved from night to day." It's at this moment that the tone changes and the poet is comforted that God's promises are true and there will yet be peace on earth. Justice will resound.

DEVOTION

Sometimes it seems hopeless. Maybe that's not what you want to read during this Christmas season, but it's true. Not every day is going to be a picnic. Some of you may be reading this even today bearing the full weight of that truth.

As long as sin continues to be present in this world, there will be conflict, turmoil, and struggle. In fact, Jesus tells us that as the day of His returning draws closer, conflict and difficulty will only intensify. It's a sobering truth. But, like this great hymn, I want to remind you that there is hope.

Ephesians 6:12 reminds us that "we do not wrestle against flesh and blood but... against the spiritual forces of evil in the heavenly places." This is a powerful truth to remember. It means the war we find ourselves in the midst of is a spiritual war, and it's bigger than us. We are powerless on our own against it— but that gives us confidence. The Lord of all creation, who sent His own Son to die for us is in charge. What could we possibly have to fear?

APPLICATION

Knowing who's in charge is only half the battle. Though the war is spiritual in nature and far above our understanding, it often still feels like we're in the trenches. It's too easy to find ourselves in conflict with one another. We feel wronged by this or that, and we want to make it right on our time. We have very little patience for the justice that God promises.

But God does indeed promise justice. Remember this season (and far beyond) that sin is our enemy. People are not. God will have His justice against the people who betray His goodness, but it's our job to love people despite their sin.

Seek peace. Seek reconciliation. Few things are as sweet as the reconciliation of God's children to each other. Sin wants to create conflict and division. God's loving plan is for peace and unity. Make unity. Do what it takes to reconcile yourself to people this side of heaven. Let God take care of the rest.

SCRIPTURE READING

Psalm 21:1-7, Ephesians 6:10-20, 2 Thessalonians 1:5-12

QUESTIONS

1. What is the source of our conflict?
2. Why can we find hope in what the true enemy is?
3. Is there a reconciliation you need to seek today? What steps can you take toward it?

DECEMBER 10TH

GOD REST YOU MERRY GENTLEMEN

God rest you merry, gentlemen,
let nothing you dismay,
remember Christ our Savior
was born on Christmas day,
to save us all from Satan's pow'r
when we were gone astray;
O tidings of comfort and joy, comfort and joy,
O tidings of comfort and joy.

From God our heav'nly Father,
a blessed angel came;
and unto certain shepherds

brought tidings of the same:
how that in Bethlehem was born
the son of God by name,
O tidings of comfort and joy, comfort
    and joy,
O tidings of comfort and joy.

"Fear not, then," said the angel,
"let nothing you affright;
this day is born a Savior
of a pure virgin bright,
to free all those who trust in him
from Satan's pow'r and might."
O tidings of comfort and joy, comfort
    and joy,
O tidings of comfort and joy.

The shepherds at those tidings
rejoiced much in mind,
and left their flocks a-feeding,
in tempest, storm, and wind,
and went to Bethlehem straightway,
the Son of God to find.

O tidings of comfort and joy, comfort
    and joy,
O tidings of comfort and joy.

HISTORY

This song has its roots deep in the middle-English era. It is one of the oldest existing carols that we have. The earliest known printing is from 1760, but there is evidence of the hymn dating back to the 16th century or earlier.

Though it's common to see the title written as, "God Rest *Ye* Merry Gentlemen", it's worth noting that the earliest 1760 publication includes the more grammatically correct "you" rather than "ye". This means that somewhere down the line, an artist rendered the text with "ye" in order to pay homage to the archaic history of the lyrics, even though the song may have never included that pronoun at all.

The song has undergone other notable changes over its lifetime, for instance, a variant printed in 1775 adapted the lyrics to better fit the style of English spoken at the time. Charles Dickens famously wrote the song into *A Christmas Carol* as the element that finally brought poor Ebenezer to redemption. As some have previously noted, this hymn is quite literally *the* Christmas carol in *A Christmas Carol*. In his story, Dickens renders the text as "God *bless* you, merry gentlemen!" (emphasis added) likely because the usage of rest had already shifted from the time the original was written.

Another version appeared in 1833 which expanded the length of the song and told more of the Luke 2 story. The additional verses served to explore more of the first Christmas from the Biblical narrative as well as the Epiphany.

Finally, one other major revision was made in 1961 and was published in "Carols for Choirs." This version retained much of the Luke 2 storytelling, but reduced the length back down to a much more digestible five stanzas.

DEVOTION

Have you ever wondered what Jesus' adult life was like? Sure, there's a lot we know about Him from Scripture, but have you ever just sat and wondered what He must have been thinking and feeling at times? I know I've had my fair share of ponderings at this. And it's hard not to. How could anyone other than God incarnate bear the weight of all our sin and shame and do so willingly and gladly?

Jesus was fully God, but He was also fully man. Surely at some point in His life He felt the gravity of His impending sacrifice for us. He knew all along what was coming, how could He not be worried about it?

Our answer to that question can really be best found in John 19 (and echoed all throughout the Bible) when Jesus is being delivered to Pilate for crucifixion. Jesus has already been beaten and scorned at this point, and starting in verse nine, seems to have a chance to get out of all of this. It's what Jesus says in this moment that reveals so much truth and beauty in suffering, its purpose, and its ultimate result in the lives of believers.

Jesus, standing before Pilate and dripping with blood, knowing that this was only the beginning of His suffering, answers Pilate: "You would have no authority over me at all unless it had been given you from above."

There it is. Tidings of comfort and joy! Our hope in every struggle, every trial, every temptation, every fear, every worry, every doubt, is that *nothing* happens that is outside of God's perfect will. From the very foundations of the Earth, God knew His plan for you—all of your deepest hurts, all of your greatest achievements, all of it—nothing surprises Him. Nothing catches Him off guard. And those who are in Christ can take comfort in that truth.

Take heart. Your suffering—no matter its depth, or weight, or amount of discomfort—is temporary, and is producing for you an eternal glory that you cannot even comprehend. Jesus knew this, and that made all the difference in what *would* have been the darkest moment in His life.

APPLICATION

It can be really tough to find comfort in times of distress. Harder still when those around us don't really know what we're going through. But take heart in knowing that you are never, ever alone in your suffering. You serve a God who loves you. And though you may suffer in this life, He has prepared a reward for you that exceeds all of your wildest expectations.

2 Corinthians reminds us that our suffering is producing something for us. We know that in the end, as Paul writes, our suffering is preparing for us an eternal glory. But what is your suffering producing for you in this life? What can you learn from it? What opportunity is it presenting?

Take the time to examine the situation you're in and see if God is trying to teach you something deeper. Even if you don't find another explicit or implicit lesson in your suffering, you still have the opportunity to strengthen your walk with Christ, by praising Him in the midst of your storm. A perfect example of this comes from Job 13:15. In the midst of Job's profound suffering, he says, "Though he slay me, I will hope in him."

SCRIPTURE READING

2 Corinthians 1:3-7, John 19:10-11, Romans 8:35-37

QUESTIONS

1. What does it mean to you to know that even in suffering, God is sovereign?
2. Think about the last time you felt like Job. That might even be today. What opportunities is your suffering presenting?

DECEMBER 11TH

WE THREE KINGS

We three kings of Orient are
Bearing gifts we traverse afar
Field and fountain, moor and mountain
Following yonder star

O Star of wonder, star of night
Star with royal beauty bright
Westward leading, still proceeding
Guide us to thy Perfect Light

Born a King on Bethlehem's plain
Gold I bring to crown Him again
King forever, ceasing never

Over us all to reign

Frankincense to offer have I
Incense owns a Deity nigh
Prayer and praising, all men raising
Worship Him, God most high

Myrrh is mine, its bitter perfume
Breathes of life of gathering gloom
Sorrowing, sighing, bleeding, dying
Sealed in the stone-cold tomb

Glorious now behold Him arise
King and God and Sacrifice
Alleluia, Alleluia
Earth to heav'n replies

HISTORY

"We Three Kings" is a dramatic Epiphany hymn that follows the narrative of Matthew 2, in which we see the wise men, or magi, bring gifts to the child Jesus. Buried in the pageantry of the familiar tune, we can extract more than a few important principles to bolster our faith.

John Henry Hopkins Jr. was the rector of an Episcopal church in Pennsylvania when he composed this familiar tune. He had very specific ideas about how the piece was to be performed. As a result, this song would become one of the more dramatic and orchestrated of the early American Christmas carols. The first and fifth stanzas were designed to be sung by all, while the middle three stanzas were written as solos, one for each king mentioned.

Though the carol specifies three kings, Scripture doesn't give us any specificity as to the number of wise men who visited Jesus. The number three comes from the three kinds of gifts mentioned throughout the prophecies found in Psalms and Isaiah, and in Matthew 2:11.

In the carol, each king takes a different aspect of Christ and His life on this earth and symbolically ties it to their gift. The first king brings gold fit for the King of Kings, the second brings frankincense as the praises and prayers lifted up to Him (Psalm 141:2), and the third king brings myrrh to foreshadow the bitter death and burial of Jesus.

All of this is wrapped in praises with a voice of hallelujah and the notion of Jesus' perfect light.

DEVOTION

The star was an unmistakable beacon to tell the coming of Christ. Many have studied, speculated, and debated the circumstances of the astrological event that led to the star's arrival, but regardless of the details, we do know the star was a light designed to point toward *the* Light.

In John 8, Jesus famously says, "I am the light of the world." When Hopkins wrote the refrain for this song, that's what he had in mind. "Guide us to Thy perfect Light," rightly recognizes that the star wasn't the important part of the narrative. The perfect Light to which it pointed was the focus.

Does the world seem dark to you? It is already dark and seems to be growing yet dimmer each and every day. Jesus predicted this would be the case as we march ever on toward His final return. We are seeing more strife between people and nations, creation is groaning for peace with more natural disasters than ever before, and our faith is being tried more than ever before.

But there is hope.

In Christ, there is light, and it is a perfect light. 1 John 1:5 reminds us, "God is light, and in him is no darkness at all."

APPLICATION

Watching the news can suck the life right out of me. When I see the depths of the turmoil and strife in this world, I often wonder when God will bring an end to the darkness. But though I don't know when He will come again, I know that He will.

The question I have to ask myself daily is: do I live as one with hope? Does the light of Christ —that "perfect Light" that Hopkins wrote about fill me with hope? To go a little deeper, is that hope infectious?

The hope that Jesus gives us with His perfect light isn't just for us. In the same way that light doesn't belong under a bushel (Matthew 5:14-16), we are designed to point people toward that perfect Light. In many ways, we are designed to be like that star from many years ago: we guide people toward Jesus.

SCRIPTURE READING

Matthew 2:1-12, John 8:12, 1 John 1:1-7

QUESTIONS

1. What can you do to live as one with infectious hope?
2. Just as the wise men brought gifts to honor a king, what can you lay before the Father in worship?

DECEMBER 12TH

THE FIRST NOEL

The first noel the angel did say
was to certain poor shepherds in fields as
*   they lay*
in fields where they lay keeping their sheep,
on a cold winter's night that was so deep.

Noel Noel
Noel Noel
Born is the King of Israel

They looked up and saw a star
shining in the east, beyond them far;
and to the earth it gave great light,

and so it continued both day and night.

And by the light of that same star,
three wise men came from country far;
to seek for a king was their intent,
and to follow the star wherever it went.

This star drew nigh to the northwest,
o'er Bethlehem it took its rest;
and there it did both stop and stay,
right over the place where Jesus lay.

Then entered in those wise men three,
full rev'rently upon their knee,
and offered there, in His presence,
their gold and myrrh and frankincense.

Then let us all with one accord
sing praises to our heav'nly Lord,
that hath made heav'n and earth of naught,
and with His blood mankind hath bought.

"The First Noel" dates to a time when carols were intended to keep the truth and message of Scripture intact through oral tradition. At the time, many were illiterate, and even if they *could* read, they would have had little access to the scriptures themselves, until the combination of two important events: the Protestant Reformation and Gutenberg's printing press.

Until those significant points in human history, carols like The First Noel would have been one of the few means of access to the Biblical narrative of Christ.

As with many of these carols, the words and tune have changed subtly over the centuries, with new stanzas being added, removed, and updated to modern English. With origins dating back to Cornwall over 600 years ago, this one is certainly not exempt from the changes of time.

The original author is unknown, and in this case, there were likely many instead of one single composer. It is a primarily an Epiphany carol, which describes Christ's birth revealed to Gentiles. The version considered to be the original contains six stanzas that tell the entire story, from shepherds to magi and their journey. In modern hymnals, we typically have 5 stanzas, using four of the originals and one newer stanza that describes all of mankind's role in Jesus' coming.

Interestingly, it would seem that if not for this carol's resurgence in popularity in the early 1800s, we may not even be singing carols today. Singing carols had largely fallen out of practice by 1823 when Davies Gilbert, concerned about the loss of tradition, published *Some Ancient Christmas Carols.* It's Gilbert who is often credited with helping to bring a revival of Christmas carols that we still love and cherish to this day.

DEVOTION

With a song so deeply steeped in tradition like this, I'm reminded of the importance of remembering. It is so important to remember how good God has been to us and to not forsake the passing down of this truth—sharing our confidence in His faithfulness with others.

In the book of Joshua, we see God do mighty things in and through the nation of Israel. We see a people wholly committed to God because of what He's done and what they've seen. Though their faith isn't perfect, by the time they have wrested the land from the Pagans to claim their inheritance, the nation boldly claims, in verse 16 of the final chapter: "Far be it from us that we should forsake the Lord to serve other gods," and then they recount the faithfulness He has shown them.

Awesome, right? Unfortunately, this story doesn't have a happy ending, which is common for the cycle of sin the nation of Israel finds themselves in for much of the Old Testament. If you turn just a page or two to the right, you'll find a sobering warning in Judges 2:10: "And all that generation also were gathered to their fathers. And there arose another generation after them who did not know the LORD or the work that he had done for Israel."

APPLICATION

What are you doing to *remember?* It seems simple, but without intentional effort, we'll find ourselves right where the nation of Israel never thought they'd be. In fact, I'd wager that if we look around the world today, we may find that verse from Judges 2 more accurate than we care to admit.

Whether it's journaling, writing songs or poetry, or making a rolodex (you can Google what that is, if you don't know) full of stories of God's faithfulness in your life, I urge you to keep His truths in front of you. And then go one step further: share the remembrance of His faithfulness with others. This could mean passing these memories down to your children. Or maybe it's finding someone to mentor and bolster their faith by sharing how God has been good to you. However you can, remember to never stop making much of what He has done for us.

Start with this holiday season: as you sing these carols of truth, remember *why* we sing.

We sing for worship and we sing for remembrance. We sing for God's glory. I encourage you to not take these songs lightly.

SCRIPTURE READING

Deuteronomy 32:7-10, Psalm 105:1-5

QUESTIONS

1. What was the intent of the early Christmas carols?
2. What are some ways that God has shown His faithfulness to you?
3. What can you do to keep the remembrance and legacy of faith alive?

DECEMBER 13TH

ANGELS WE HAVE HEARD ON HIGH

Angels we have heard on high
Sweetly singing o'er the plains
And the mountains in reply
Echoing their joyous strains
Gloria in excelsis Deo!
Gloria in excelsis Deo!

Shepherds, why this jubilee?
Why your joyous strains prolong?
What the gladsome tidings be?
Which inspire your heavenly songs?
Gloria in excelsis Deo!
Gloria in excelsis Deo!

Come to Bethlehem and see
Him whose birth the angels sing;
Come, adore on bended knee,
Christ the Lord, the newborn King.
Gloria in excelsis Deo!
Gloria in excelsis Deo!

See Him in a manger laid,
Jesus, Lord of heaven and earth;
Mary, Joseph, lend your aid,
With us sing our Saviour's birth.
Gloria in excelsis Deo!
Gloria in excelsis Deo!

HISTORY

This is one of the rare exceptions in any catalog of Christmas songs that seems to be relatively unchanged over the course of its life. It is believed to have been written in the 18th century, and its first known publication was in 1843. Originally published in French, under the title *Les Anges dans nos campagnes* which literally translates to "the angels in our countryside," it was later adapted to English in 1862 by James Chadwick, a Catholic bishop at the time in England.

The English version is true to the French version in some sections, and loosely translated in some others, but the overall message of the song remains constant. The most iconic line in the song—Gloria in excelsis Deo—is Latin for the song's main message, taken directly from Luke 2:14—Glory to God in the highest.

DEVOTION

When was the last time your praise made someone stop and take notice? I don't mean because of your beautiful voice or your choice of classic hymns, but because of genuine, heartfelt praise, poured out to Christ our King? When was the last time that someone asked you, like the shepherds, "why this jubilee?" We know that the Bible tells us many times in many places the value and the importance of offering our praises to God, but many times, when life gets busy and chaotic, this can be one of the first things we forget.

If we look back to the latter part of 2 Chronicles 5, Solomon has just finished building the temple, the Ark of the Covenant is brought in, and "King Solomon and all the congregation of Israel" were gathered to sacrifice. There is rejoicing and people are in high spirits about the new temple. But then we see something really awesome right at the end of this chapter.

"and when the song was raised, with trumpets and cymbals and other musical instruments, in praise to the LORD, 'For he is good, for his steadfast love endures forever,' the house, the house of the LORD, was filled with a cloud, so that the priests could not stand to minister because of the cloud, for the glory of the LORD filled the house of God."

You read that right! Their praise was so powerful, so pleasing to God that His spirit filled the temple like a cloud, so overwhelming that the priests couldn't even stick around. They had to exit the temple because of God's presence.

APPLICATION

With all the hustle and bustle that the Christmas season brings—Shopping, cooking, decorating, kids musicals, getting together with friends and loved ones—it's easy to lose sight of the reason for our praise—God in the flesh, brought down as a sacrifice for us so that we can dwell with Him in eternity. But as you conquer the last minute sales and put the finishing touches on the fruitcake remember to turn everything back to God as praise. This doesn't just mean in song, either.

When the person behind you at the supermarket is grouchy, show them the loving-kindness that Christ has shown you. When someone cuts you off in traffic, extend the same grace that Christ did to you. When your kids make you late for your work Christmas party, just sing your favorite Christmas songs, and forgive them as Christ forgave you. The Spirit of God probably won't manifest as an all-consuming cloud around you, but the peace of God will be evident with you.

Is your praise infectious? Does it make people take notice? Does it inspire others to cry out in worship? Worship is not just the 20 minutes of music before the message at church on Sunday. Worship is an attitude. Is your attitude worshipful?

SCRIPTURE READING

Philippians 2:12-18, 2 Chronicles 5:2-14, Hebrews 13:15

QUESTIONS

1. What would you tell someone who stopped you and asked, "Why this jubilee?"
2. Would you describe yourself as having a worshipful attitude? Why or why not?
3. What are some ways (besides songs) that you can pour out your praise to Him?

DECEMBER 14TH

O COME ALL YE FAITHFUL

O come, all ye faithful, joyful and
    triumphant!
O come ye, O come ye to Bethlehem;
Come and behold him
Born the King of Angels:
O come, let us adore Him,
Christ the Lord.

God of God, light of light,
Lo, he abhors not the Virgin's womb;
True God, begotten, not created:
O come, let us adore Him,
Christ the Lord.

Sing, choirs of angels, sing in exultation,
Sing, all ye citizens of Heaven above!
Glory to God, glory in the highest:
O come, let us adore Him,
Christ the Lord.

Yea, Lord, we greet thee, born this happy
  morning;
Jesus, to thee be glory given!
Word of the Father, now in flesh appearing!
O come, let us adore Him,
Christ the Lord.

HISTORY

This hymn has a storied history that at times reads more like a spy movie than the history of a beloved Christmas carol.

The words are often credited to John Francis Wade, who was an Englishman exiled to France after the failed Jacobite rebellion of 1745. Some legends would hold that this hymn is actually a coded message for those members of the rebellion. Some manuscripts that Wade transcribed are decorated with Jacobite floral patterns and maybe even coded Jacobite messages.

Recent discoveries point to another author who precedes Wade by a century: King John IV of Portugal. The king was also known as "The Musician King" and composed many works of his own. He was something of a modern David, at least in the intersection of royalty and song-writing.

Whether politically motivated or intended as a carol of praise for Christ at His birth, the content of the carol is still sound and the call to action is no less compelling for us today: "O come let us adore Him!"

DEVOTION

This song brings up a big question for us today: what does it mean to adore Him? How do we adore God?

I'm wired to be a very practical, hands-on, and tactile person. I sometimes struggle with abstract concepts such as adoration. How does one express adoration? It's not a very concrete principle to wrap the mind around. You can't see it, touch it, or feel it, so how do you know if you're doing it right?

These are the kinds of questions I find myself asking all too often.

It turns out the answer may be easier than I thought—as usual, I tend to overcomplicate things.

Fun fact: the word *adore* never appears in the Bible. We do, however, have terms like exaltation, praise, honor, and even more colorful expressions of adoration, such as one found in Psalm 2: "kiss the Son."

The truth is, God is the only one worthy of our praise, and worthy of far more praise than we can ever give. In scriptures like Revelation 5:12, we see that He is worthy of so much more than we have to offer—but we can offer our hearts.

APPLICATION

Okay, but *how* do we express adoration? How do we offer our hearts?

Fortunately, the Bible has no shortage of scriptures on the subjects of praise, exaltation and honor, which today's reading will reflect. But the simplest way to think about it may be to look at the third definition of adore, according to Webster: "to be very fond of".

So there's at least one really easy way to express adoration for God: tell Him how much you love Him. That's a great place to start, and the rest will follow.

This season is all about Jesus coming to us, stepping into our world, and redeeming us from our sin and from ourselves. He came to us and now we have an opportunity to come to Him. Spend some time truly praising Him this season—build up a habit that carries you through to January and beyond.

Truly adore Him. Express your fondness. Tell Him how awesome He is and mean it. O come let us adore Him!

SCRIPTURE READING

Psalm 8, Psalm 148

QUESTIONS

1. What does it mean to adore God?
2. What does adoration look like to you?
3. How can you be in the habit of adoring Him daily?

DECEMBER 15TH

THE HYMN OF JOY

Joyful, joyful, we adore Thee
God of glory, Lord of love
Hearts unfold like flow'rs before Thee
Op'ning to the Sun above
Melt the clouds of sin and sadness
drive the dark of doubt away
Giver of immortal gladness
fill us with the light of day

All Thy works with joy surround Thee
Earth and heav'n reflect Thy rays
Stars and angels sing around Thee
center of unbroken praise

Field and forest, vale and mountain
Flow'ry meadow, flashing sea
chanting bird and flowing fountain
call us to rejoice in Thee

Thou art giving and forgiving
ever blessing, ever blest
well-spring of the joy of living
ocean-depth of happy rest
Thou the Father, Christ our Brother—
all who live in love are Thine
Teach us how to love each other
lift us to the Joy Divine

Mortals join the mighty chorus
which the morning stars began
Father-love is reigning o'er us
brother-love binds man to man.
Ever singing, march we onward
victors in the midst of strife
joyful music lifts us sunward
in the triumph song of life

I f you're not wholly familiar with the name of this song, as soon as you see the first two words, your mind likely needs no help humming the rest of the familiar tune. Though not quite as old as other additions to this collection, The Hymn of Joy—often known as "Ode to Joy" or "Joyful Joyful We Adore Thee"—is perhaps one of the most familiar and timeless melodies for those in English-speaking parts of the world.

The story of this hymn is well-documented. It was written in 1907 by Henry van Dyke with the intent to sing to Beethoven's Ode to Joy, the final movement of the composer's famous 9th Symphony.

Against the backdrop of mounting tensions in Europe—the early rumblings of The Great War, what would be known as World War I—van Dyke found joy and beauty in the Berkshire Mountains in western Massachusetts. Though there is little about the hymn that is specifically related to the Christmas story, it echoes other

Christmas carols in expressing joy and adoration for the God of glory.

Henry van Dyke would later discuss the hymn, remarking that part of his message behind the words is to instill a trust that science can do no harm to religion—the idea that if you observe the majesty of God's creation, as Romans 1:20 reinforces, you shouldn't be surprised that there is a Creator. According to van Dyke: "this is a hymn of trust and joy and hope."

DEVOTION

Take a look around you for a moment. If you're inside, perhaps find a window. Look at a tree or a cloud or a mountain if you're blessed to live within view of one. The world is teeming with life and beauty and purpose. There is majesty in the very creation of this universe. Doesn't that alone make the Creator worthy of adoration?

Isaiah 49:13 reminds us that creation is bursting to exalt the Lord. Everything around us—everything we see and touch and feel and sense is designed to point us back to Him. This is a vibrant world He has created, and it points to a vibrant God who is worthy of all our praise. If the rocks and the trees and the stars cry out to God, to lavish their joy on Him, should we not do the same?

We are the darling of His creation, created in His image to have a relationship with Him. How joyful is that truth?

APPLICATION

When you see the beauty of this world, you ought to be reminded of the Creator. When you marvel at a breathtaking moment, direct that praise toward the Lord. Colossians 1:16 says, "For by him all things were created, in heaven and on earth, visible and invisible, whether thrones or dominions or rulers or authorities—all things are created through him and for him."

All things are created through and for Jesus. This same Jesus humbled Himself so much to step down into His creation as a helpless babe. He was mocked, ridiculed, slandered, disrespected, beaten, and finally murdered by those

He created. Through His defeat of death, He adopted His rebellious children as co-heirs of the grace purchased by His blood.

This is the Jesus we celebrate when we look at the beauty of the world. This is the King we sing praise to this holiday season. In the face of such overwhelming grace and provision, how could we do anything else?

SCRIPTURE READING

Psalm 19, Isaiah 55:10-13, Colossians 1:15-23

QUESTIONS

1. What are some reasons you have to praise and adore the God of creation?
2. Do you think we deserve to experience the beauty of creation given to us by God? Why or why not?
3. Why can we celebrate with joyful adoration during this season (and all seasons)?

DECEMBER 16TH

THE MESSIAH: HALLELUJAH CHORUS

Hallelujah

For the Lord God omnipotent reigneth
Hallelujah

The Kingdom of this world
Is become
The Kingdom of our Lord
And of His Christ
And of His Christ

And He shall reign forever and ever

King of Kings (Forever and ever hallelujah
  hallelujah)
And Lord of Lords (Forever and ever
  hallelujah hallelujah)

And he shall reign forever and ever (And he
  shall reign)

King of Kings forever and ever
And Lord of Lords hallelujah hallelujah
And he shall reign forever, forever and ever

King of Kings and Lord of Lords
King of Kings and Lord of Lords
And he shall reign forever and ever (And he
  shall reign forever and ever)

Forever and ever, forever and ever (King of
  Kings and Lord of Lords)

Hallelujah

There is something immediately regal and celebratory even in the first few notes of this tune. You know it immediately. If you grew up steeped in tradition, you may even be tempted to jump to your feet before the first four notes have sounded. It's simply that iconic.

The Hallelujah Chorus (along with the rest of the Messiah oratorio) was written as a libretto by Charles Jennens in 1741. In case you're as confused by Italian operatic terms as I was when I started this journey, an oratorio is like an opera, except intended to be more of a concert piece than musical theater. It's a concert with a message instead of acting, essentially. And a libretto is the text used for oratorios, operas, musicals, etc.

The story goes that Jennens handed the libretto to Handel in the summer of 1741 and just 24 days later, George Frideric Handel had finished composing the entire 260-page oratorio.

After a stunning premiere the following

Easter season in Dublin, enthusiasm for the piece waned but by the end of the 1740s, the oratorio had solidified itself in the public's favor, due in part to the inclusion in fundraising events, like the annual London's Foundling Hospital fundraiser concert, of which Handel was a huge supporter.

Somewhere along the way, the piece migrated from Easter to become the Christmas staple we all know and love today.

DEVOTION

The lyrics to this part of The Messiah oratorio are fairly simple and repetitive. And that's really not a bad thing. The redundancy by no means robs the piece of its power.

There is something incredibly powerful about shouting, "Hallelujah" to the Lord. The word itself is a Hebrew word meaning "God be praised." Now, imagine with me, a world in which we all boldly sing "God be praised!" at the top of our voices, and we all mean it.

The words from this oratorio come straight

from Scripture, with this section primarily lifted from Revelation 19. This setting is important. It depicts such a bright future for us.

I think much of the power from this song is that we get a glimpse of what it might look like at the end of all things when for all eternity all the saints and the heavenly host will sing "Hallelujah" in the presence of God. Even Handel himself reportedly told a servant after his 24-day writing stint: "I did think I did see all Heaven before me, and the great God Himself seated on His throne, with His company of Angels."

The song goes on to repeat that, "He shall reign forever and ever, hallelujah," and I can't think of a better reason to praise.

APPLICATION

Christ came to reign. And not just to reign over us, that we should be mindless servants bent to His will. He came for a relationship with us. He came to adopt us as children that we can be called friends and children of God.

This time of year, we celebrate the birth of Christ. He first came in humility to purchase salvation for His children. Our hope now is that He will return again as a conqueror. This isn't a hope in something wished for, this hope is in expectation of a promise fulfilled.

1 Corinthians 15:26 reminds us, "The last enemy to be destroyed is death." It is in this setting that we see the chorus of eternal "Hallelujah" and in this truth we can put our trust and hope.

So this season is a time of remembrance and celebration for what Christ has done for us, but don't let it stop there. This is also a season of joyful expectation and celebration of the fact and promise that Christ will return and with Him, final victory over sin and death. If that doesn't make you want to jump out of your seat and shout, "Hallelujah!" I don't know what will.

SCRIPTURE READING

Revelation 19, 1 Corinthians 15:20-28

QUESTIONS

1. What does the word hallelujah mean to you?
2. Why should God's omnipotent (all-powerful) reign give you hope?
3. Are you making the most of every moment in expectation of Christ's fulfilled promise? Why or why not?

DECEMBER 17TH

HARK! THE HERALD ANGELS SING

HARK! the Herald Angels sing
Glory to the new-born King!
Peace on Earth, and Mercy mild,
God and Sinners reconcil'd.
Joyful all ye Nations rise,
Join the Triumphs of the Skies;
Nature rise and worship him,
Who is born at Bethlehem.

Christ by highest Heav'n ador'd,
Christ the everlasting Lord;
Late in Time behold-him come,
Offspring of the Virgin's Womb.

Veil'd in Flesh the Godhead see,
Hail th' incarnate Deity!
Pleas'd as Man with Men t'appear,
Jesus our Emmanuel here.

Hail the Heav'n-born Prince of Peace
Hail the Sun of Righteousness!
Light and Life around he brings,
Ris'n with Healing in his Wings.
Mild he lays his Glory by,
Born that Men no more may die;
Born to raise the Sons of Earth,
Born to give them second Birth.

HISTORY

The story of the carol we sing today is absolutely fascinating, not to mention the fact that it would have been a nightmare if the modern copyright system were in play. In fact, the original author might have been able to hum this tune as it plays through the speakers at his local grocery store and never know he was singing his own song.

In 1739, a recently converted Charles Wesley wrote this hymn titled, "Hymn for Christmas-Day" with a little bit of a different opening line than you might expect. The song started, "Hark! how all the welkin rings, Glory to the King of Kings" but Wesley's friend, George Whitfield would later change the opening lines to the familiar two lines we get today.

When Wesley penned the words, he imagined it being set to slow and solemn music, likely so that the singer or listener could soak in and absorb the depth of the lyrics he wrote—which is understandable, the lyrics are incredible.

Sweet, poignant statements such as "Pleas'd as Man with Men t'appear, Jesus our Emmanuel here," may be a little unfamiliar for our modern publications, but the words certainly aren't lacking in comfort or power.

Over a century after it was initially written, William H. Cummings adapted the words to a secular tune that would become the most familiar version of the music we know today. The festive, celebratory music we can all sing off the top of our head is a far cry from the solemnity Wesley initially envisioned, but it is certainly fitting of the Christmas spirit we've all come to love.

DEVOTION

Why did Jesus come?

That's a loaded question, isn't it? Jesus gives us a little insight in John 3:17 when He's discussing this idea of a "second birth" with a Pharisee named Nicodemus. "For God did not send his Son into the world to condemn the world, but in order that the world might be saved through him."

That's a pretty big deal. See, the secular worldview of our faith wants to preach the false gospel that Jesus (and by extension, God) is a judgemental, condemning fairy tale. But we know that isn't true. We've experienced the goodness that Jesus brings to us through His death, burial, and resurrection.

Jesus didn't come here to condemn and

judge His children. He came to bring salvation and freedom. This song reminds us that He was, "Born to give [us] second birth."

It's a weird concept to understand, this idea of being born twice. But it's a principle we must appreciate—the idea of being made entirely new, through Christ.

APPLICATION

The newness is what we celebrate this season. For one, we sing, "glory to the new-born King!" but it doesn't stop there. We celebrate the new life Christ has given us.

For some of you, this might be your first Christmas as a believer, and all the familiar songs and traditions have an exciting new meaning for you. For others, this might be just another Christmas, another in a long line of traditions you enjoy observing with your family every year.

My prayer for you is that the Gospel will come alive to you in new and amazing ways. We have a lot to celebrate. We get to celebrate a

God who saves, not one who condemns. You've heard it called the Good News, and there is a fantastic reason for that: the news is *good*.

The churchy word for this is the "ministry of reconciliation," and it's the idea that the sinner is saved by the Sinless One. Where once there was unresolvable conflict, there is now reconciliation.

Take time to celebrate the reconciliation. Take time to thank God, and to ask Him for forgiveness. Reconcile yourself to God this season and take part in the joy that He brings.

SCRIPTURE READING

John 3:1-21, 2 Corinthians 5:11-21

QUESTIONS

1. What are some comforting truths you can celebrate today?
2. What does the "ministry of reconciliation" mean to you?
3. How does being made a new creation affect your daily life?

DECEMBER 18TH

GO TELL IT ON THE MOUNTAIN

Go, tell it on the mountain,
Over the hills and everywhere
Go, tell it on the mountain,
That Jesus Christ is born.

While shepherds kept their watching
Over silent flocks by night
Behold throughout the heavens
There shone a holy light.

The shepherds feared and trembled,
When lo! Above the earth,
Rang out the angels chorus

That hailed the Savior's birth.

Down in a lowly manger
The humble Christ was born
And God sent us salvation
That blessed Christmas morn.

HISTORY

We don't know who originally wrote these words, and we likely never will. That's not to say its history isn't fascinating, however.

The words were officially compiled and published in the early 1900s by John Wesley Work, Jr, a choir director, educator, and Harvard alum. He's also credited as being the first African-American collector of African-American spirituals and folk songs. It is as part of one of these collections that "Go Tell It on the Mountain" originally appeared.

At the turn of the century, Work embarked on the difficult challenge of collecting the folk songs and spirituals from the fields of the south and immortalizing them. Without his endeavors with his wife and brother, many of the folk songs which marked a darker time in American history may have been lost forever. Now, an important piece of culture and history is preserved in volumes like Work's own, "New Jubilee Songs and Folk Songs of the American Negro."

DEVOTION

Does the idea of going and telling sound familiar? It should. Some of Jesus' last words before being taken up to heaven at the end of His ministry were to give the disciples one last command: "Go therefore, and make disciples of all nations, baptizing them in the name of the Father and of the Son and of the Holy Spirit." (Matthew 28:19)

The words from this song are lifted straight from a few places in Scripture. Perhaps obviously, the narrative from Luke 2 of the shepherds being interrupted in their fields by the angels proclaiming the coming of the King. But the chorus is taken from Isaiah 40:9, "Go up to a high mountain, O Zion, herald of good news."

This song serves as a great reminder of the Christmas story, but it is so much more than that. It's a reminder of our calling and purpose; it's a reminder of the reason God doesn't whisk us away to heaven the moment we're saved. We are to proclaim the Good News of the God who came in the mildest form to bring us salvation.

APPLICATION

Why should we go tell it on the mountain? Well, for one, God considers those blessed who share the Good News: "How beautiful upon the mountain are the feet of him who brings good news," comes from Isaiah 52 in the midst of a powerful prophecy about the Lord's coming salvation.

But we want other people to experience the joy of salvation as we have experienced it. We want those we care about to share in the freedom which comes from the sacrifice of Christ.

We're not in the business of changing people. We don't get a raise based on the converts we bring into the fold—we are hope dealers. It's not about getting people to act like us, it's about seeing people freed from the chains that bind them. In some cases, they may not even know that they are bound. Should we not, then, endeavor to share the news that what is bound can be free?

When you sing Christmas songs, say Merry Christmas, or hum glad tidings, remember that it can and should go much deeper than that. This is a season of jubilee—don't keep it to yourself. Preach Christ and the salvation that has come through Him. Let this season be a season of new birth for someone else. It's the best Christmas gift you can offer.

SCRIPTURE READING

Isaiah 40:1-10, Isaiah 52:7-10, Matthew 28:16-20

QUESTIONS

1. Can you remember a time when someone else faithfully shared the Gospel with you?
2. When is a time you've been prompted to share the Gospel with someone?
3. How will you be intentional this season in sharing the Good News?

DECEMBER 19TH

GLORY BE TO GOD ON HIGH

Glory be to God on high,
And peace on earth descend;
God comes down, He bows the sky,
And shows Himself our Friend!
God th'invisible appears,
God the Blest, the Great I AM,
Sojourns in this vale of tears,
And Jesus is His Name.

Him the angels all adored,
Their Maker and their King;
Tidings of their humbled Lord
They now to mortals bring;

Emptied of His majesty,
Of His dazzling glories shorn,
Being's Source begins to be,
And God Himself is born!

See th'eternal Son of God
A mortal Son of Man,
Dwelling in an earthly clod
Whom Heaven cannot contain!
Stand amazed, ye heav'ns, at this!
See the Lord of earth and skies
Humbled to the dust He is,
And in a manger lies!

We, the sons of men, rejoice,
The Prince of Peace proclaim,
With the angels lift up our voice,
And shout Immanuel's Name;
Knees and hearts to Him we bow;
Of our flesh, and of our bone,
Jesus is our Brother now,
And God is all our own!

The history for this hymn is rather light. It was written by Charles Wesley, and when you've written over 6,000 hymns, they can't all have a moving backstory. This by no means detracts from the power of the lyrics or the truth of what they say.

Interestingly, if you do a search for this song by Charles Wesley, you may come up with two different results. One result is a general hymn of praise for who God is, while the other is more distinctly related to the incarnation of Christ and meditates on the angel's praise of God in flesh.

The most popular tune set to this hymn in the western hemisphere is called AMSTER-DAM, while it seems eastern and Russian orthodox choirs prefer the German tune ELLACOMBE.

The influence for these words is obviously extracted from the Luke 2 narrative and explore an unique perspective: what must it have been like for the angels to see their omnipotent God whom they have worshiped long now laid low in the form of His creation? The second stanza especially explores this idea. Another influence seems to be Solomon's prayer of dedication for the temple in 1 Kings 8.

DEVOTION

For the majority of human history, there has been a separation between us, God's creation, and the fulness of His glory. When Moses was allowed to experience a shadow of God's glory, Moses had to hide and veil his face from His presence. In fact, so radiant was God's glory that Moses had to veil his face before the other Israelites could even look at him. And Moses was mostly hidden from the full glory of God! Just by being in the vicinity of God's glory, even the side-effects of God's power were too much to behold.

Then, 2,000 years ago everything changed. The glory of God rested in humble dust. In the person of Jesus Christ, God in flesh came to dwell with man. By the power of the incarnation and the blood poured out on the cross, God's glory became approachable.

As Jesus breathed His last, the veil was torn —both the literal veil in the temple of that day and the veil over our hearts. The glory of God came in power and blessed humility and changed *everything*.

APPLICATION

In 2 Corinthians 3, Paul refers to the "ministry of death," that is, the condemnation that comes from the standard set by the law. But by the power of Jesus, we are now members of the ministry of the Spirit and "where the Spirit of the Lord is there is freedom." (2 Corinthians 3:17)

What does this mean for us today? Now that the fulness of the glory of God has descended on us through His Spirit, we are being transformed. And there is freedom in that divine transformation!

No longer are we striving in vain against the bridle of the letter, that is, the Law. The Spirit who gives life transforms us. There is no longer separation between the glory of God and His creation. We can rest in that truth. No longer do we toil and strive for atonement, but Jesus has purchased that redemption by His blood, and by the power of the purchase, the Holy Spirit transforms us into His image. We can rest in that, because Jesus' yoke is easy and His burden is light.

It's easy to wonder if we're good enough for the ministry God has placed before us. Make no mistake, if you are a believer, God has placed a ministry before you! You know what's awesome? Since God has seen fit to place His glory in us, *we* don't have to be good enough. Christ in us is good enough, and that is all we need. Rest in that truth today. Rest in the transforming power of God and give glory to God on high.

SCRIPTURE READING

1 Kings 8:12-30, 2 Corinthians 3

QUESTIONS

1. Do you believe you're good enough for the ministry God has placed you in?
2. How do you daily seek the radiant glory of God?
3. Why can we have confidence in God's calling on our lives, despite our own limitations?

DECEMBER 20TH

WHAT CHILD IS THIS?

What Child is this who, laid to rest
On Mary's lap is sleeping?
Whom angels greet with anthems sweet,
While shepherds watch are keeping?
This, this is Christ the King,
Whom shepherds guard and angels sing;
Haste, haste, to bring Him laud,
The Babe, the Son of Mary.

Why lies He in such mean estate,
Where ox and ass are feeding?
Good Christians, fear, for sinners here
The silent Word is pleading.

Nails, spear shall pierce Him through,
The cross be borne for me, for you.
Hail, hail the Word made flesh,
The Babe, the Son of Mary.

So bring Him incense, gold and myrrh,
Come peasant, king to own Him;
The King of kings salvation brings,
Let loving hearts enthrone Him.
Raise, raise a song on high,
The virgin sings her lullaby.
Joy, joy for Christ is born,
The Babe, the Son of Mary.

HISTORY

Penned by William Chatterton Dix in 1865, this song began its life as a poem titled, "The Manger Throne." In 1865, Dix was overcome with a severe and unexpected illness which left him bedridden, burdened with severe depression, and which nearly claimed his life. During this time, Dix underwent a personal spiritual revival, spending a significant amount of time reading his Bible, and writing several hymns, including "Alleluia! Sing to Jesus!" and "As with Gladness Men of Old."

This classic hymn, though written in 1865, wasn't published until 1871 when it made its appearance in "Christmas Carols Old and New," a publication in the United Kingdom which featured a collection of carols. This publication was edited by Henry Ramsden Bramley and John Stainer who together teamed up to curate and compose scores for some of the most iconic Christmas hymns. It is not known for certain who was responsible for adapting the verses of Dix's poem into this classic Christmas song, but it is believed that it was likely John Stainer who paired these stanzas with the tune of "Greensleeves."

DEVOTION

Who among us hasn't suffered some sort of personal tragedy? Whether it's the death of a loved one, the loss of a job or a severe illness that you think you'll never make it through—all of us have suffered. And if you haven't, you will. It's just one of the inevitabilities of life. We shouldn't be surprised by this, though. God literally told us right up front at the fall of man in Genesis that things were going to be tough for us. It seems, though, that many times stories like Dix's are inspired by some great personal tragedy. Something awful happens, and *then* he turns to Christ, is struck with profound reverence for His glory, and gives Him praise for it.

But why do we wait? Why do we wait for tragedy? Why does circumstance dictate when we praise God? Or more importantly, why does circumstance dictate when we *don't* praise him?

The joy and peace that come from remembering and acknowledging God's grace and sovereignty at all times is a thread that is intimately woven into Scripture. One of my favorite examples is Paul in the book of Acts.

At one time, Paul was one of the most aggressive persecutors of the Church, until God changed his heart.

Paul goes on to share the Gospel all over, all the while being pursued and persecuted in the same manner that he had done to believers just a short time before. But Paul, in his weakest moments, continues to bring praise to God. In fact, it's repeatedly the first thing he does! In Acts 16 — Paul and Silas have just been arrested for their interactions in Philippi. "About midnight Paul and Silas were singing hymns to God, and the prisoners were listening to them." (Acts 16:25). Then through an awesome series of events (I won't spoil it for you, go read it yourself) the jailer that had been guarding them was saved, and he too returned the glory to God!

In his darkest moments and in his finest hours, we often see the first thing Paul does is give glory back to God. And so should we. Haste haste to bring Him laud! You're not Goldilocks. Don't wait until things are "just right" to give God the glory that He deserves. In every moment of every day, give Him praise.

APPLICATION

We exist to bring praise to God, no matter our circumstances. Whether you're on the highest peak or in the lowest valley, God owes you nothing but deserves everything.

As you walk through your day, be intentional about finding opportunities to praise God. And remember that praise is not just the 20 minutes before the sermon on Sunday morning. We bring praise to God in many ways.

Hebrews 13:15-16 says "Through him then let us continually offer up a sacrifice of praise to God, that is, the fruit of lips that acknowledge his name. Do not neglect to do good and to share what you have, for such sacrifices are pleasing to God."

In the jail cell, Paul shared the peace that he had found in Christ. As a result, the jailer also gave his life to Christ and gave praise to God. In the same way, we can be a light that guides someone to Christ's redemptive glory by continuing to praise Him at all times.

SCRIPTURE READING

Psalm 145, Acts 16:25-34, Isaiah 9:2-7

QUESTIONS

1. What are some things in your life, right now, that you can give God praise for?
2. How do your interactions on social media bring praise to God? If they don't, how can you change that?
3. What can you do to develop a more praiseful attitude in any situation?

DECEMBER 21ST

AWAY IN A MANGER

Away in a manger, no crib for a bed,
The little Lord Jesus laid down his sweet
   head.
The stars in the bright sky looked down
   where he lay,
The little Lord Jesus asleep on the hay.

The cattle are lowing, the baby awakes,
But little Lord Jesus, no crying he makes.
I love thee, Lord Jesus! look down from
   the sky,
And stay by my cradle till morning is nigh.

Be near me, Lord Jesus; I ask thee to stay
Close by me forever, and love me I pray.
Bless all the dear children in thy tender care,
And take us to heaven to live with thee there.

HISTORY

The first time this hymn appeared was in 1882 titled "Luther's Cradle Song." The publisher included the first two stanzas and attributed it to Martin Luther, claiming he'd written the hymn for his children and that mothers in Germany sing the lullaby to their children still. There is little evidence to support this claim, however, as none of Luther's work bears any semblance to this carol, nor are there any German texts for the carol from before 1934, and even those texts read more like a translation *to* German, rather than an original source.

Ten years after the first publication of stanzas one and two, a third stanza appeared, though credit for this addition is equally ambiguous and disputed. Thus, the true authorship and origins of this hymn remain anonymous.

In addition to disputes over the authorship of the hymn, the theological precision of the hymn has come under the microscope. The issue revolves around the intent of the second verse, "But little Lord Jesus, no crying He makes." Opponents to the hymn will claim that the lyric implies docetism, which is a fancy word for the belief that Jesus' humanity wasn't real, but He instead only *resembled* a natural-born man.

DEVOTION

The phrase "little Lord Jesus" presents a fascinating dichotomy. It's such a gentle way to express the humility of the Christ—that the Son, divine member of the Godhead, would step into human form. Not only that, but as a helpless baby with "no crib for a bed."

And why? Why did the Savior, God in the flesh, come in this fashion?

It's all about nearness. Which is exactly what

this lullaby prays for in the last two stanzas. It's powerful and important to remember that the God we worship isn't a distant, apathetic deity who abuses His authority. Hebrews 4:15 gives us this great confidence: "For we do not have a high priest who is unable to sympathize with our weaknesses, but one who in every respect has been tempted as we are, yet without sin."

Why is this a boon to our confidence and comfort? We need only consult the next verse: "Let us then draw near to the throne of grace, that we may receive mercy and find grace to help in time of need."

The sweet truth is that we have a God whom we can relate to. We have a relationship with a God who was like us, only perfect in every way. Because of this, He knows what we've been through. He has felt what we have felt. This powerful truth makes way for a nearness that nothing else in this world can offer.

Christmas is now only days away. For some, you may simply need to rest in the truth and knowledge that Jesus is *near.* We've discussed the difficulty of approaching this season in times of loss or grieving. But as Christmas Day approaches closer, more and more traditions that will never be the same serve only as a reminder of the emptiness and grief we feel.

We look for reasons to celebrate, but find only more reasons to grieve and hurt. It's not uncommon to feel alone or maybe empty, as all around us the world celebrates with holiday cheer.

Have comfort, believer. Jesus is near. It may take a truly herculean effort to let yourself rest in that truth, but know that it is true. Jesus experienced true pain and true loss and even wept (John 11:35) in His grief! He understands us. He understands hurt.

Take time today to make the last stanza of this sweet little children's carol your prayer: "Be near me, Lord Jesus; I ask Thee to stay close by me forever and love me I pray."

SCRIPTURE READING

Isaiah 41:18-29, John 11:1-44

QUESTIONS

1. Why did Jesus come in the humble form of a baby to live as a human?
2. Why should Jesus' humanity come as a confidence and comfort to us?
3. How are you struggling this Christmas season? Write that down and give it to Jesus today, because He understands all your struggles!

DECEMBER 22ND

GOOD CHRISTIAN MEN REJOICE

Good Christian men rejoice
With heart and soul and voice!
Give ye heed to what we say
News! News!
Jesus Christ is born today!
Ox and ass before Him bow
And He is in the manger now
Christ is born today!
Christ is born today!

Good Christian men, rejoice
With heart and soul and voice
Now ye hear of endless bliss

Joy! Joy!
Jesus Christ was born for this
He hath ope'd the heav'nly door
And man is blessed evermore
Christ was born for this
Christ was born for this

Good Christian men, rejoice
With heart and soul and voice
Now ye need not fear the grave:
Peace! Peace!
Jesus Christ was born to save
Calls you one and calls you all
To gain His everlasting hall
Christ was born to save
Christ was born to save

HISTORY

With many of the exceptionally old songs on our list, it is difficult to track down a specific year (or even place, or person in some cases) of authorship for them and this mostly has to do with the fact that many of these songs were written in a time before there were reliable records, or before people were reading and writing. This song is no exception. Likely written sometime in the 1300s, this may be the single oldest song on the list.

Originally titled In Dulci Jubilo, this song began its life as a traditional Christmas carol written in Latin and German. The original title translates to "In Sweet Rejoicing."

It is believed that the original song was written by Heinrich Seuse in 1328. It seems that little else is known about the song's origin, or inspiration, but German folklore holds that Seuse's inspiration for the song came from an interaction with angels in which he heard them sing the lyrics and joined them in dance.

The first known printed version of the song is in a German codex which now resides in the library at Leipzig University in Germany.

Although adapted to different languages several times over its lifetime, the central message of this song remains the same: give God praise for all that He's done!

Jesus' life is woven with humble threads from the very beginning. What is the single most common piece of imagery we see this time of year? Baby Jesus lying in a manger among the various farm animals in the quaint township of Bethlehem. The King of Kings stepped down from Glory to dwell among us and did so in a manner completely unexpected for someone so worthy of glory.

All throughout Jesus' life, from His birth, until His death, we see Him interacting with, loving, and blessing the very least that society had to offer. The lepers, the tax collectors, the beaten, bruised, and broken—no one was beneath Him. No one in the path of Jesus' ministry on Earth was too lost, or too broken, or too lowly to be loved and served by Him.

Just as the song says in that second verse— He hath opened the heavenly door.

We serve a God who loves us. A God who paid the ultimate price for us, whether we deserved it or not (spoiler alert: we didn't!)

APPLICATION

God loves you. Read that again. Let it sink in for a minute.

Maybe you're walking through a season of heartbreak. Maybe you've done some things you're not proud of. Maybe you just don't feel like you're all that special.

The truth is, God loves you.

He loves you so much that He gave His Son for you. He loves you so much that before the very dawn of time, He knew everything about you. He knew exactly who you would turn out to be. He knew every single mistake you would ever make (Hebrews 4:13). And still, He sent His son to be the ultimate sacrifice for you. Don't miss the beauty of that.

It's hard to find a better example of this throughout the Bible than in Paul.

Paul was one of the leading persecutors of Christians during his time. But following his conversion, he becomes one of the greatest agents of faith in the Bible, helping to establish the Church all across the land. But Paul wasn't a solo artist—we see time and time again that God's divine purpose surrounded him. In 1 Timothy 1:12-14, Paul says "I thank him who has given me strength, Christ Jesus our Lord, because he judged me faithful, appointing me to his service, though formerly I was a blasphemer, persecutor, and insolent opponent. But I received mercy because I had acted ignorantly in unbelief, and the grace of our Lord overflowed for me with the faith and love that are in Christ Jesus."

If God can love, redeem, and use Paul—a man who so violently attacked and opposed His people—then what makes you think He can't love, redeem, and use *you*? Let go of your past, and run to the God who made you, who called you, and who loves you.

SCRIPTURE READING

1 Timothy 1:12-17, 2 Corinthians 4:8-18, Psalm 51:1-12

QUESTIONS

1. What things are holding you back from a genuine relationship with God?
2. Why do we sometimes feel unredeemable?
3. What can you do right now to step out of your past, and into His mercy?

DECEMBER 23RD

O HOLY NIGHT

O holy night! The stars are brightly shining,
It is the night of our dear Saviour's birth.
Long lay the world in sin and error pining,
Till He appear'd and the soul felt its worth.
A thrill of hope, the weary world rejoices,
For yonder breaks a new and glorious morn.

Fall on your knees! O hear the angel voices!
O night divine, O night when Christ was
   born;
O night divine, O night, O night Divine.

Truly He taught us to love one another;

His law is love and His gospel is peace.
Chains shall He break for the slave is our
*   brother;*
And in His name all oppression shall cease.
Sweet hymns of joy in grateful chorus
*   raise we,*
Let all within us praise His holy name.

Christ is the Lord! O praise His Name
*   forever,*
His power and glory evermore proclaim.
His power and glory evermore proclaim.

HISTORY

The story of this carol is fascinating. In fact, I never would have guessed a single story could combine an atheist poet, a Jewish composer, a carol banned by an entire country, an abolitionist, and the advent of radio broadcasting, but this carol delivers.

As the story goes, a parish in a small French town wanted to commemorate the grand opening of their newly renovated organ with a poem and a song in 1843. So the parishioner asked a local wine merchant and poet, Placide Cappeau to write a Christmas poem for the Christmas Eve service. Cappeau wasn't exactly known for his church attendance, but he gladly took on the task and, after ruminating on Luke 2, penned these words.

Cappeau would later ask his friend and composer, Adolphe Adam to compose the music, who, though he was Jewish and didn't believe in Christ as the son of God, obliged. Adam wrote the music for a soprano he knew, Emily Laurey. The song, "Cantique de Noël," took hold in the hearts of the French people, and became something of a holiday anthem for the country.

Unfortunately, Cappeau would renounce the church and anti-Semitism would take root, which led to the French Catholic church summarily banning the song nationwide as "unfit." The song would make its way across the Atlantic to be translated by a Unitarian minister and abolitionist named John Sullivan Dwight. The translation bears marked differences from its French counterpart and the English lyrics as a whole are not without theological difficulty, but this beautiful picture of the soul's worth warrants discussion.

DEVOTION

The greatest theological difficulty with this song is the idea of a night being holy or divine. Though Dwight's borderline pantheism (the belief that God is *in* everything) makes its way into the song through these ideas, we can operate on the notion that a divine night simply means the power of what happened that first Christmas proceeded from God and changed everything for all of His children.

Despite the trouble with one or two parts of the song, all the beauty of the Gospel is found in these two lines: *"Long lay the world in sin and error pining, / Till He appear'd and the soul felt its worth."*

This is such a powerful reminder of the Gospel. When sin entered the world, strife and turmoil abounded, and we were stuck in it. We were powerless to free ourselves from the bondage of our separation from God. But there was a promise. There was a pursuit. In Christ, God demonstrated how much we are worth to Him. Spoiler alert: it's a lot.

In Isaiah 53, one of the most famous Messianic prophecies reminds us, "He was pierced for our transgressions, he was crushed for our iniquities; upon him was the chastisement that brought us peace, and with his wounds we are healed."

The empowering, humbling, and liberating truth of Christmas is this: Jesus stepped down from heaven—fully God and yet fully man—and was mocked and humiliated in every way by His own creation, His body battered and bruised to the point of an excruciating death. Did you know the word "excruciating" refers to the specific torment of the Roman cross?

Jesus endured all of that to save His people. That's how much your soul is worth to your heavenly Father: the life of the perfect spotless Lamb of God. Don't neglect the gravity of that truth this Christmas season.

APPLICATION

This time of year is a great time of reflection on the birth of Christ, and to remember that God stepped into our world to save us. But context is important. The beginning of this story is fruitless without the end of the story. To fully measure the impact of Christ's birth, we must consider the power in His death and resurrection.

In the life of Christ we have a new birth—in the death of Christ we have eternal life. Jesus defeated death by charging through its very doors and emerging victorious, broken chains in hand. This is a season of remembrance for our freedom from sin and the bondage of death.

Christmas is the first act in a story that would change *everything*. The first steps of the infant Jesus were the first steps on His long journey to the tomb where He would prove that there is no power on Earth or in Hell that can stop Him. That's how much your soul is worth.

SCRIPTURE READING

Isaiah 53, Luke 23:1-49

QUESTIONS

1. How can you celebrate Christmas 365 days a year, not only this month?
2. The cradle was a journey to the cross. Why is it important to remember both this time of year?
3. In your own words, how much is your soul worth?

DECEMBER 24TH

SILENT NIGHT

Silent night, holy night,
All is calm, all is bright
Round yon virgin mother and child.
Holy infant, so tender and mild,
Sleep in heavenly peace,
Sleep in heavenly peace.

Silent night, holy night,
Shepherds quake at the sight;
Glories stream from heaven afar,
Heavenly hosts sing Alleluia!
Christ the Savior is born,
Christ the Savior is born!

Silent night, holy night,
Son of God, love's pure light;
Radiant beams from thy holy face
With the dawn of redeeming grace,
Jesus, Lord, at thy birth,
Jesus, Lord, at thy birth.

HISTORY

Originally titled *Stille Nacht, Heilige Nacht* (which literally translates to "Silent Night, Holy Night"), this song was written by Father Joseph Mohr in 1816, and the music composed by Franz Xaver Gruber two years later in 1818.

The song was originally performed in a church in what is now present day Austria where Mohr worked. Following the performance, the man who serviced the church's organ, Karl Mauracher, was completely taken with the piece and took a composition back home with him to Tyrol, Austria. From there, it changed hands several times, being performed in many various places before making its way into the American zeitgeist in 1839. Some small changes were made to the melody around this time, giving life to the version we know and love today.

And love it we do!

The single recorded by Bing Crosby in 1935 is the fourth best selling single of all time at about 30 million copies sold.

DEVOTION

It's Christmas Eve, the fast paced shuffle of this season is nearly behind us. Maybe you have a few more family gatherings to go to or another Christmas party to attend, but by now things are settling down, and we're settling in with our families.

In many traditions, this is the time families gather and read through the Luke 2 narrative. Candlelight services are usually found in abundance. In many ways, we collectively unite as a single Church to solemnly sing this very song.

Although short, this song does a wonderful job of painting the scene of peace and serenity that follows Christ. In every verse some reference is given to peace, and calm, and tenderness.

And what a perfect time for a reminder like this. After everything that this season and even this year has brought us to, and through, this is a perfect time to reflect on the peace that we have when we rest in Jesus. Peace like that of Jesus in the storm (Matthew 8:23-26, Mark 4:35-39, Luke 8:22-24). Peace that, in the midst of our darkest, most challenging moments, stands up and says to our fears "Silence! Be Still!"

APPLICATION

For some of us it's been a tough year. In fact, for most of us, there have probably been some moments of turmoil this year. And oftentimes, the Christmas season is a painful reminder of some of those struggles.

But, take heart in knowing that our God has conquered every fear of sin and death. And just like with the winds and the waves, He silences our struggles.

When we look throughout Scripture for evidence of the peace that surrounds God's presence, it's hard to turn a page without coming up with something. And many great examples are concentrated around Jesus' life and ministry. In fact, even in His final days, He was still sharing a message of peace with His disciples. In John 14:1, Jesus tells the disciples "Let not your hearts be troubled. Believe in God; believe also in me."

And it really is just that simple.

You may still hurt. You may still grieve. You may be scared out of your mind about things. But there is an undeniable peace that follows you when you pursue God.

SCRIPTURE READING

Matthew 6:25-34, Philippians 4

QUESTIONS

1. How has God shown you His peace in previous situations?
2. When the storms come, how can you remember this supernatural peace?
3. How can walking in God's peace help you face current or future situations?

DECEMBER 25TH

JOY TO THE WORLD

Joy to the World; the Lord is come!
Let earth receive her King!
Let ev'ry heart prepare Him room,
And Heaven and nature sing.

Joy to the earth, the Savior reigns!
Let men their songs employ;
While fields & floods, rocks, hills & plains
Repeat the sounding joy.

No more let sins and sorrows grow,
Nor thorns infest the ground;
He comes to make his blessings flow

Far as the curse is found.

He rules the world with truth and grace,
And makes the nations prove
The glories of His righteousness,
And wonders of His love.

HISTORY

Few notes celebrate the joy of Christmas Day quite like the opening triumph of *Joy to the World*. When that bold proclamation rings out, it's impossible to not *feel* the excitement of the song. It's considered the most published Christmas song in the U.S. and as a result, there are versions for every taste and style. The song truly speaks of Christmas, and there is simply no better way to describe the feeling of Christmas Day.

The writer of this exuberant hymn is Isaac Watts, the famously prolific English hymnist. Watts wrote this hymn in 1719 as part of a collection of his own poetry based on the Psalms. The intent of his book, *The Psalms of David: Imi-*

tated in the language of the New Testament, and applied to the Christian state and worship, was to illustrate that the redemptive story and the power of Scripture comes not from isolated incidents, but from one broad narrative. In short, all Scripture must be viewed through the correct lens: The Gospel.

Watts' intent with "Joy to the World" was never to write a Christmas song, but to create a modern retelling of Psalm 98 in poetry. The poem would later be set to various tunes before Lowell Mason's ANTIOCH became the popular choice. Mason borrowed melody elements from Handel's "Messiah" compositions, including the very first four notes which are so triumphant and captivating, even in their simplicity.

Though Watts never intended for this song to be an advent carol, it has become a favorite anthem for the coming of Christ for centuries.

DEVOTION

Watts based his poem on Psalm 98, which is very much a tale of two parts: we celebrate the joy of God's revelation and realization of our salvation, and then we delight in looking forward to the final judgement, after which Jesus will rule His people in goodness and truth. Even the intent of Watts, with his *The Psalms of David* project was to illustrate that the redemptive story is necessarily two parts. So it follows that "Joy to the World" would, in itself, speak of two very important events and tie them together with joy.

"Joy to the World" dwells not only on the coming of Christ, but on the salvation Jesus brought and then His final judgement and reign. We celebrate today because Jesus stepped into the world in humility—and all creation exclaimed in joy. But the story doesn't stop there. We celebrate because Jesus came to bring salvation to "no more let sins and sorrows grow" but in their stead, joy and peace. Finally, even in victory on the cross, Jesus didn't stop there. He's coming back, and with Him final victory, final glory, and the fullness of His wondrous love.

APPLICATION

In Psalm 98:2, David identified the source of his joy: "The Lord has made known his salvation; he has revealed his righteousness in the sight of the nations." In fact, the entirety of Psalm 98 describes the broader narrative of God's redemptive plan through Jesus. What does this mean for us today? Christmas is not only something we celebrate between Thanksgiving and New Years, but instead we celebrate the joy of the Gospel each and every day.

In that light, "Joy to the World", as well as the whole of the Christmas story describes a gift far bigger and far sweeter than any temporary thing. You've heard the cliche about a "gift that keeps on giving." The story of the Gospel is a widespread and eternity-reaching narrative that touches every single soul.

Some advent calendars and family traditions employ a similar method of gift-giving: there isn't one gift, but instead a progression of gifts over a period of time. Typically all of these gifts will circle around a certain theme or tell a broader story.

As we unwrap gifts and connect with family and friends, remember that the gift of Jesus' life that brings us together today is just the start of something special. The baby in the manger is but the first gift in a master plan that leads to the cross and opens the door for a sinful people to know God.

Joy to the world, the Lord is come!

SCRIPTURE READING

Psalm 98, Hebrews 9:19-39

QUESTIONS

1. Why is it important to remember that Jesus' birth was just the first act in a powerful redemptive story?
2. What promise from Jesus do we have to look forward to?
3. What Jesus started at Christmas, He finished at Easter. How will you devote daily time to the celebration of that truth in the months between now and then?

SCRIPTURE INDEX

Psalm 51:1-12

Psalm 98

Psalm 98:2

Psalm 105:1-5

Psalm 124:8

Psalm 126

Psalm 136

Psalm 141:2

Psalm 145

Psalm 148

Isaiah 7:14

Isaiah 9:2-7

Isaiah 11:1-11

Isaiah 26:1-12

Isaiah 35:1

Isaiah 40:9

Isaiah 40:1-10

Isaiah 41:18-34

Isaiah 49:13

Isaiah 52:7

Isaiah 52:7-10

Isaiah 53

Isaiah 53:5

Isaiah 55:10-13

John 11:1-44

John 14:1

John 16:32-33

John 19:9-11

Acts 16:25

Acts 16:25-34

Romans 1:20

Romans 5

Romans 8:35-37

1 Corinthians 1:23

1 Corinthians 15:26

1 Corinthians 15:20-28

2 Corinthians 1:3-7

2 Corinthians 3:17

2 Corinthians 3

2 Corinthians 4:8-18

2 Corinthians 5:11-21

Galatians 4:4-5

Ephesians 1:3-10

Ephesians 2:10

Ephesians 6:12

Ephesians 6:10-20

Philippians 2:10-11

Philippians 2:12-18

Philippians 4
Colossians 1:16
Colossians 1:15-23
2 Thessalonians 1:5-12
1 Timothy 1:12-14
1 Timothy 1:12-17
Hebrews 4:13
Hebrews 9:19-39
Hebrews 13:15
James 1:16-18, 22-25
1 John 1:5
Revelation 5:12
Revelation 19

Claim Your Free Devotional Gift

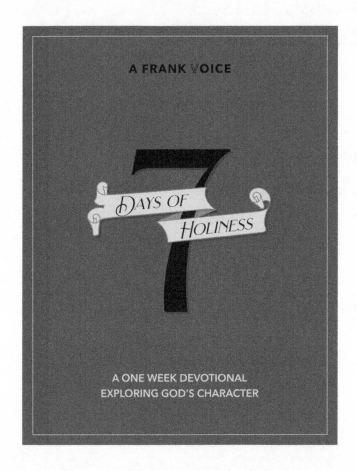

Transform the Way You See Holiness

Claim your **free** *7 Days of Holiness* devotional
from A Frank Voice at
www.7daysofholiness.com

ACKNOWLEDGMENTS

PRESTON

I would like to thank my co-author and one of my best friends, Cameron Frank for allowing me to be a part of this process, and showing me how much I simultaneously enjoy writing but loathe the process. It's been a ton of fun to write this with you, Cam. I look forward to our future projects, if you can stand to let me work on anything else with you, ever.

I'd like to thank my mom and my grandmother (and the many others who came before them) for being pillars of the faith in our family.

Without them dragging me to church and remaining faithful in sharing the gospel with me while I was just a heathen little kid, I no doubt wouldn't be who I am today, and I certainly wouldn't have written a word of this book. Love you mom and grandma!

I'd also like to thank my dad who taught me the meaning and value of hard work. Without everything I learned from him, I would have walked away from this book in the first 15 minutes of research. The countless hours spent at Starbucks early in the morning, and at my desk late into the night would never have happened if I hadn't grown up with such a great example of tenacity. Love you, dad!

I would like to thank my wife, Katelyn, for being so flexible and understanding while I've worked on this. For tackling bedtimes and bathtimes by herself at times so I could keep writing, for giving me crucial, real-time feedback on my writing, and for no doubt praying alongside me throughout this project. I love you, babe!

Finally, I would like to thank the many

scores of friends and family that have supported this project all along the way. Your prayers and excitement over this book have been instrumental in keeping me going during the long nights and early mornings.

CAMERON

It may seem obvious, but without Jesus, everything else is meaningless. If not for my Savior intervening in my life, I would have no hope—indeed, no worth. The fact that I can discuss the power of redemption today is solely because Jesus redeemed a sinner such as me. No trifle feat.

My wife has always been my biggest supporter and my greatest advocate, no matter the adversity. Hailee, you are so good to me! Thank you for letting me take the time to work on this and other projects I get myself wrapped up in.

Preston, thank you so much for putting up with my overbearingness. I wouldn't challenge you if I didn't believe in you. Thank you for being a part of this project and dedicating your time and energy to making it awesome. You're one of the greatest guys around and I'm honored to call you one of my very best friends.

To my Phoenix Fiction Writers, your incredible prayer and support while I take a detour from fiction has been invaluable to me. You guys are awesome, and it's hard to imagine getting anywhere without your support!

It's hard for me to separate Christmas from memories with my family. You have all been so supportive of all my shenanigans through the years. I know this Christmas will be tough, but we have each other, and we know what Christmas is all about. To my parents: thank you for showing the spirit of Christ in Christmas, even when some years were tougher than others. To my sisters: thank you for modeling humility and joy in every circumstance. To all my other friends and family who have helped me, encouraged me, and supported me: thank you, thank you, thank you.

ABOUT

ABOUT PRESTON

At work, Preston is a full-time software sales rep, at home he's a full-time father of 3 beautiful little girls, and husband of one beautiful wife of 9 years.

Preston's wife often tells him that his biggest hobby is collecting hobbies. In his free time, he enjoys, but isn't very good at, hunting, fishing, hiking, ham radio, stamp collecting, home renovation, tinkering with electronics, graphic design, photography, lawn care, and probably just about anything else that constitutes a hobby.

He loves the Lord with all his heart and lives to serve His kingdom.

ABOUT CAMERON

Cameron Frank considers himself a professional dabbler. He loves to create. He knows a little bit about a lot of things, and a lot about almost nothing. When he isn't fixing printers and fielding questions about the volume of worship music, he's a writer, musician, designer, and the Director of Media at Cherokee Hills Baptist Church.

He loves the Lord, and he cherishes his family. He lives in Oklahoma City dodging tornados with his beautiful wife, Hailee and their two sons.

Go deeper than the hymnal and learn the inspiring and encouraging stories behind the hymns you know and love. Connect the words of the hymns to Scripture in a unique and thought-provoking way.

Each week is structured to take you through a specific element of the Father's character and reflect on Him: Creation, Grace, Faithfulness, and Worship.

Each day will focus on a different hymn, including the hymn's text, a brief history and testimony about the hymn, and a devotion based on truths found in the hymn and corresponding Scripture.

WORD IN HEART

Scripture memory is one of the most important disciplines a Christian can master. It's an imperative that we see all throughout Scripture and a practice that can change the life of the believer.

In Word in Heart my goal is to make the purpose, impact, and practice of Scripture memory as accessible as possible. You will learn some tips, tricks, and resources that I use every single day to memorize the Word of God.

I truly believe we can experience revival if a people unite in the diligent practice of internalizing the truths and treasures in the Word of God. Your journey starts today.

WORD IN HABIT

Do you want to finally build a consistent and meaningful quiet time habit? It's hard to do, but you can learn tips and practices today that will set you up for an enduring personal Bible study habit.

In Word in Habit, we explore why the Bible is important, what to expect when you read the Scriptures, and how to extract important principles to apply to your daily life.

You'll find suggestions for different ways to study, including **five** different application tools to try, with suggestions for how they might fit into your daily practice.

THE WORD IN HABIT JOURNAL

The Bible is the most important book ever written. It is transformative and powerful, living and active, and a clear look into the heart of God. But it can be difficult to apply to our daily life.

A great way to approach the application of the

Scriptures is through the habit of journaling. Something about finding a way to put things into words helps us wrap our minds around a thought or idea and really cement it. It can be difficult to start, though. When you stare at that blank page and wonder what in the world to put there, it can do the opposite of help you apply the text—it can cause you to freeze up.

The Word in Habit Journal is designed to help guide you and give you direction in your approach to applying Scripture.

BREAKING BARRIERS

By Stefan Johnsson

You were created with a purpose. You exist to be a light in your community, a reflection of Christ to those around you.

As globalization makes the world feel smaller and brings cultures closer together, it might be easy to feel overwhelmed or uncomfortable.

Our reflex might be to place barriers between ourselves and diversity, but the gospel compels us to break down these barriers and illuminate the world with the light of Christ. The truth is that this mixing of cultures creates an opportunity for the advancement of the gospel like never before.

This is a call to action and a challenge for you—not to blame you or shame you for inaction, but to empower you with the gospel truth so that you can seize the mission field on your very own doorstep.

Breaking Barriers is a personal and practical guide to help you understand and interact with cultures different than your own. Stefan brings a fresh, personal perspective to remind you what the Bible is already telling you to do.

Made in United States
Orlando, FL
29 November 2021